FIND YOUR PACE

Emma Kirk-Odunubi is a gait analyst, footwear expert and Sports Science graduate with over fifteen years of experience in the running industry. Day to day, she works with a variety of sportspeople, from the novice runner to the elite athlete. She's been an ambassador for major global brands, including Puma, Under Armour and lululemon, and is no stranger to a challenge herself. From 15+ marathons and multiple half marathons to indoor Ironman events and 24-hour fitness fundraisers, Emma walks the talk (or runs it, rather).

EMMA
KIRK-ODUNUBI

FIND YOUR PACE

How Running Changed My Life
and How It Can Change
Yours Too

BLUEBIRD

First published 2026 by Bluebird
an imprint of Pan Macmillan
The Smithson, 6 Briset Street, London EC1M 5NR
EU representative: Macmillan Publishers Ireland Ltd, 1st Floor,
The Liffey Trust Centre, 117–126 Sheriff Street Upper,
Dublin 1 D01 YC43
Associated companies throughout the world

ISBN 978-1-0350-6279-9

1 3 5 7 9 8 6 4 2

A CIP catalogue record for this book is available from the British Library.

Typeset in Trade Gothic by Palimpsest Book Production Ltd, Falkirk, Stirlingshire

Printed and bound in the UK using 100% Renewable Electricity by CPI Group (UK) Ltd

This book contains the opinions and ideas of its author. It is intended to provide helpful general
information on the subjects that it addresses. It is not in any way a substitute for the advice of
the reader's own doctor(s) or other medical professionals based on the reader's own individual
conditions, symptoms or concerns. If the reader needs personal medical, health, dietary, exercise
or other assistance or advice, the reader should consult a competent physician and/or other
qualified health care professionals. The author and publisher specifically disclaim all responsibility
for injury, damage, or loss that the reader may incur as a direct or indirect consequence of following
any directions or suggestions given in the book or participating in any programmes described in the
book. The reader is advised not to undertake, cease or modify any treatments, diets or health
procedures without consulting a professional. Failure to adhere to this recommendation may
result in adverse health impacts, for which the author and publisher accept no responsibility.

Visit **www.panmacmillan.com/bluebird** to read more about
all our books and to buy them.

This book is dedicated to those willing to try.
Those willing to try and to fail and to learn.
Learning is how we build knowledge.
And knowledge is your superpower.

CONTENTS

INTRODUCTION

There are moments in your life when everything changes. Moments that might seem small, but which set you on course for a whole new journey. One of mine? An evening in Victoria Park, London, surrounded by over 5,000 women, all wearing matching teal vests and t-shirts. There was a buzz of energy in the air. The evening was cool, crisp and alive with the collective anticipation of what lay ahead. It was back in the day when headphones were still allowed in races, and women clutched MP3 players and phones and fiddled with the wires of their headphones, ensuring they were perfectly untangled. I knelt down, tugging at my laces for the third or fourth time, to make sure my trainers were secure – just in case I hadn't checked properly. I'd heard stories of friends' shoelaces coming undone mid-run, and although part of me thought a pit stop might be a welcome reprieve, I wasn't about to risk it. My heart was already racing. *Was I really about to run a whole 10 kilometres?*

No one had warned me about the chaos before a race. The bag drop was a logistical puzzle – a swarm of sweaty, agitated strangers rushing, afraid of missing the start of the run.

Endless queues for the toilets. A surreal combination of anxiety and camaraderie. It reminded me of the women's bathroom at a nightclub at 2 a.m., as strangers struck up conversations, shared last-minute pep talks and complimented each other's kit.

'Oh, I love your shoes! Where did you get them?' one woman said to another.

'That jacket looks amazing – it's such great material.'

Laughter and chatter filled the air as if we were old friends, though most of us had never met before. There was an atmosphere of anticipation for what the future would hold once we all took our first steps. Strangers became cheerleaders, offering words of encouragement.

'How are you feeling? You're going to be amazing!' one woman said, her smile contagious. 'You've got this. Just enjoy it. Have fun!'

The positivity was overwhelming. It felt like these women all believed in me more than I believed in myself. After peeing for the third time – more out of nerves than necessity – I walked towards the start line. My stomach was doing backflips – like the moment on a rollercoaster when the barriers drop and the ride starts moving, and you realize it's too late to get off. The start line loomed ahead and I took a deep breath, steadying myself. I was really about to run this.

I looked around and saw I wasn't the only one feeling the pressure building. On my left, a woman bounced up and down on the spot, as if trying to propel herself off the ground. Giggling, distant whooping and hollering filled the air – we were all getting hyped.

One woman made direct eye contact with me and, beaming, said, 'What *are* we doing here?'

'No idea!' I said with a sheepish side-eye.

We both laughed, wished each other well, and then she was gone, weaving through the crowd like a fish in water. My heart pounded in my chest. My palms were slick with sweat, a sticky reminder of the tension coursing through me. Before I could stop myself, I started bouncing on my toes too, desperate to shake off the restless energy building within me. As I walked to the start line, I thought: *That woman was right. What was I doing here on the start line of my first-ever race?* This wasn't a space I was used to occupying. I knew sport — the netball court, a throwing circle; they'd been my arenas for over ten years, the places I knew and understood. Not this. Not running. Not since I was a kid. I used to make fun of runners I saw when I was at the athletics track throwing. I'd question why they'd spend their time simply running round in circles. But here I was, surrounded by a sea of women coming together to celebrate our ability to move and run as one. Here I was — a runner.

This race was a space to bring women together to run at night, to feel safe and celebrate along the way. The slogan on the Nike website read:

We work hard and run harder. Live fast and run faster. We run on adrenaline, on friendship, on love. We. Just. Run. We are girls inspired. We own the night. It's more than just a race. It's a movement. Rally your crew, run your city and own the night.

The focus wasn't on speed or performance. The main aim of this run was to build community – to bring people together. I'd been searching for community, craving it, since I'd moved to London, and in this moment, I was about to be part of something greater. I was going to own it.

The start line glowed like a beacon, draped in a dazzling array of neon lights. A teal-green border of light traced the path ahead like a luminous guide, drawing us towards where everything would begin. The air carried the freshness of a post-rain British summer evening: warm, inviting and invigorating. Nostalgic millennial dance tracks blared from the speakers, their pounding beats weaving into the buzz of excitement around me. As I focused, all I could hear was my own breath, quickening more than I'd like it to. I tried to ground myself, closed my eyes, put my headphones in and let the music cocoon me from the outside world. I wiggled my toes inside my running shoes, feeling their snug, familiar grip, holding promises of speed and strength. My pulse surged, a burst of energy radiating through me as I opened my eyes and fixed my gaze ahead. This was it – my first race. It was time.

'Three . . . Two . . . One . . . GO!'

At the moment of setting off, with spectators whooping and my music pushing me forwards, it was like I'd drunk rocket fuel and taken off into orbit. This pace was short-lived, but the run route was glorious, through the park, which now boasted blue skies. As we entered the second half of the race, night fell and the light installations along the course came alive. Neon pinks, greens and purples lit the path as the sky darkened. I'd made it halfway. I was doing it.

The last 3km, however, were brutal. I began to pay for my jet-pack-fuelled start. It felt like cement bricks were attached to my feet. Sweat coated my body; my lips felt sticky and tasted salty. My form was non-existent as I flailed my arms like someone drowning. I'd hoped my spirited effort would make me faster and get me to the finish line a little quicker. I turned the last narrow corner, scuffing my heels, and the final 100 metres appeared. I channelled my inner Usain Bolt and tore towards the line. *Run tall. Proud chest. Yes, you can.* I threw my hands in the air as I crossed the finish. I'd done it. Every single part of my body hurt. Even though I could barely catch my breath, and even though I'd wanted to sit down and stop during those final kilometres, never to do it again, I knew I'd be signing up for another race. This would not be my last. I had conquered my mind and pushed my body in a way I hadn't felt before. Running this race had changed me.

You may think that running is simply a form of exercise, a way to stay fit. And that is true, but I've written this book to show you there's more to running than burning calories. Running has brought so much more into my life than physical changes. It's helped me to overcome the most traumatic times in my life. In these pages, I'll introduce you to the secrets of one of the strongest relationships I have, one that I've built through running: my relationship with myself. I'll show you how you can find this for *yourself*, too. You'll see how I, Emma – a regular person – have battled mental health issues, the loss of loved ones, loneliness and identity issues, yet continue to show up on the road, lacing up my shoes because of how running makes me feel.

A warning, though. I'm not here to convince you that running will be easy. I'd be lying if I said that were true. It *shouldn't* always be easy. When runs are hard, they become a foundation for growth. When they become easier, they're a mark of progress. Physical and mental resilience are built through this process.

I'm here to teach you what I've learned from running so far — as well as what I'm still learning. I've processed difficult emotions and grief by putting one foot in front of the other. I've discovered that the possibilities of what I can achieve are greater than I could have ever imagined. I've found running to be a comfort — a safe space for me to think, learn and grow. And I'll teach you how to do it too: from how to progress your pace, to the science of choosing the right running shoes, to building strength, and all the injury prevention in between. I'll take you where I've been — as a running coach with decades of experience and as a gait analyst, who has assessed thousands of different runners; as a younger me, earning my sports science degree and my strength and conditioning qualification; as a child, running for fun, as a way to feel free before I lost touch with it as a teenager; and, most importantly, as a runner — as a person. I'll share the knowledge I've collected over the years and how you can apply it to your own journey. I want to show you how running has shaped me and pushed me forwards in life, one step at a time.

Running is a feeling — a sensation that exists somewhere between having control over yourself and surrendering to the ground beneath your feet. It's the way your breath can become a meditative, steady *inhale, exhale*, making the stresses of the world shrink. Running is a conversation with yourself. Running is freedom, and I want you all to be able to enjoy it for your entire life, using this book not only as your guide but also as a reminder that running is for *you*. Every runner is valid, no matter your starting point or pace. This book is a helping hand for you to navigate your goals, wherever you are in your running life. Are you ready to run towards yourself, to find out who you really are and allow running to be the vehicle to help you get there?

I want to show you that starting to run, and finding intention and motivation behind your runs, can bring you infinite positive possibilities – not just to your life in the broader sense, but also to each day, week and month. I want to show you how I learned to run *towards* rather than away from myself, and encourage you to do the same.

Back at the race, with my pulse pounding like drums in my ears, the medal was placed around my neck. Like a queen receiving her crown, I stood tall, pride and elation radiating from within. I was worthy of this victory. Every shift of the medal against my chest was a reminder of the journey it represented – the self-doubt on cold, dark mornings, the long, lonely miles where quitting felt easier than continuing.

This medal was proof. Proof that I had fought, endured and conquered. Proof that I was capable – more capable than I ever believed. Sure, the race gave me a shiny reward, but was it essential? No. That I had pushed myself, achieved something I didn't know I could do – that was my real proof. Running no longer felt like a punishment; it was a test of limits. And I felt so free.

PART 1
WHY I RUN

Running is a never-ending encyclopaedia of lessons. It's not just the simple, physical matter of sweating a lot, burning through calories or collapsing in a heap at the end – that's only part of the story.

There are many different reasons why you might want to run, and understanding those may be the kicker you need to get started, stick at it or improve your pace, endurance or distance – whatever goal has brought you to this book. In Part 1, I'll share what I've learned at each step. I'm going to let you know how growing up, and some of the tricky challenges I've experienced, shaped me; how they've brought me back to running; and how those runs have helped. Sadly, some of these experiences, I know, are pretty universal.

Whoever you are, I want you to feel seen in these pages.

In Part 2, I'll share in detail the *how* – running tips, training plans and more, to get you started or help you improve. But first, I'm going to take you through the *why*. I'll share what my motivations have been – what's driven me to consistently lace up my trainers and go running – and, in the process, let's see if you can identify what yours might be.

Ready. Set. Go!

FINDING ADULTHOOD

To understand how running changed my life, you first have to understand who I am. As you read this book, you'll learn how my relationship to running evolved as I grew up, and how my reasons and motivations to run changed with it. There were years in my young adulthood when I didn't run at all, and then I rediscovered the joys of it – but as a child, running was simple.

I was known for always having energy. I was like a shaken-up can of sparkling drink that overspills when you try to open it. I was excited to explore and seek out the fun in every single day. My mum tells me that this effervescence was constant, beginning when I first learned to walk.

'You used to run away from your dad and me down the street,' she told me recently. 'We would coerce you back by offering you biscuits and tasty snacks. We knew we couldn't catch you, firstly, and also – we knew you loved your biscuits.'

Some things don't change; I'm still an energetic, die-hard snack fan. But more importantly, as a child, I *loved* to run. When I was five years old, I believed that if I ran fast enough, I'd fly. My arms would flail with reckless abandon, laughter flooding out of my mouth mid-stride, all the energy buzzing inside me being used. Running was magic.

I also loved school. I channelled all my extra energy into learning, and school was where I first discovered my love of sport – specifically running. My teacher in Reception was head of the cross-country and athletics club, and helped nurture my passion for sport. You had to be seven years old to join the athletics club, but even at four I was desperate to be part of it. I was like a golden retriever puppy, bouncing around every day in the flat, the streets and the garden, playing with my friends, then toys, then friends again. Running and sport helped me release that overflowing zest for movement, and I fell for it hard.

I still remember my first day at the school athletics club. The clock struck 3.15 p.m., and I bolted to the toilets with my PE kit in hand and changed out of my uniform – dropping my school tie, then my socks, into my bag – before darting to the meeting point. I waited in the school hall, the deep-brown wooden floor an enormous puzzle underfoot, while the off-white walls, marked with old Blu-Tack stains, told stories of countless music sheets and artwork displays. The smell of lunchtime meals still wafted from the kitchen, mingling with the faint metallic tang of the hall's gymnastics frames folded against the walls. Those frames, every child's dream to climb on, stood silent witness to our bodies humming with restless vigour. Today, though, it was about running.

I was one of only a couple of girls at the after-school club – the rest were older boys. We warmed up inside with high knees, fast feet and pogo jumps, and then the teacher talked us through the route around the school grounds. I was apprehensive about being one of the only girls but trusted myself and my legs. When she blew the whistle, we began. As soon as the sound hit my ears, I shot out like a greyhound.

From that very first after-school run, I was determined not just to keep up with the boys but to beat them. My top chasing target was a boy called Charlie Grice. Sound familiar? Charlie (now retired) is an Olympic, World, Commonwealth and European finalist for Great Britain in the 1500m. I just knew him as the boy I could never catch. I didn't mind. I was competitive, but whatever the result, I felt like the warm summer sun was shining on me every time I ran (even in heavy rain). The more I ran, the more I found that I was actually good at it, and this realization only increased the joy it brought me. I achieved some local top-ten finishes in races, and loved the thrill of overtaking my competition, chasing them down like prey. But that really wasn't my main motivation. Even then, I understood that I continued to run because running made me happy. That sunshine feeling warmed me every time I laced up my shoes. I'd found a way to feel connected to myself through the simple act of movement.

One of my earliest memories of seeing someone who looked like me in sport is when Kelly Holmes won the Olympic bronze medal for the 800m in the year 2000. I was eight, and it meant everything to me. And then in 2004, she won one of two Olympic gold medals in a thunderous 800m final against Maria Mutola. I was on the edge of my seat as the camera panned across to her: rocking her braids, her shoulders broad, chest proud, eyes staring past the camera like a hawk. The stadium was silent. At home, we all moved closer to the screen, and then the gun went off. From watching Kelly in previous races, I knew her tactic. She would run at the back of the pack at first, giving the other athletes a false sense of security. Then, she'd pass them, one by one, as she ran the rest of the race. Kelly edged Maria out for the win in the last 20m. She had done it. Double Olympic champion. As I watched her cross the line, I threw my arms in the air and leapt to my feet.

'YESSSS!' I screamed, looking at my mum clapping at the television. As I saw someone with brown skin achieving excellence, I said to Mum: 'I want to be just like her.'

At school, I was aware there weren't many people who looked like me. It was more of a subconscious awareness, but I could see the differences in my hair and my skin. In school photos, I was not only the tallest – usually right in the middle of the back row – but one of two out of thirty students who weren't white. I had some mixed-race friends who I had met at nursery, and my mum actively made sure we kept in touch. She understood the importance of me feeling seen while growing up. Sport was one of the main areas of life where the colour of my skin – according both to society and my own eyes – was seen as an advantage. Black people within sport were largely celebrated. I watched athletes who looked like me succeeding in the Olympics. I felt seen in the running space. Not only did seeing Kelly win encourage me to start sports training seriously, but it also drove home for me something I believe to this day: you can't be what you can't see. In Kelly Holmes, I saw possibility for me.

Kelly Holmes' bronze medal inspired me to join another athletics club, which, in classic Emma style, I did as soon as I was able – no waiting around. With my teacher's guidance, I became part of Brighton Phoenix at nine years old – a now very well-established running club that helped and encouraged me to enter local races, train and compete in multiple running events. But the more I competed, the more I realized how many other runners were quite a bit better than me. At that point, running was still only about competition, success and being the best. I was pretty good, but I wanted to be *great*. Secretly, I wanted to go to the Olympics. I loved the idea of being the best at something and all that came with it – performing on a global stage, signing with the biggest brands and becoming someone others could look up to, like Kelly Holmes was for me. Sport was already my obsession, so why not dream big?

At nine years old, I didn't understand the work it would take, but that's the beauty of a dream. You don't need the full road map. You just need the spark – and I had it.

Running was my starting point, but I found myself wanting to try other sports too. What did I have the potential to be great in? Although I still loved the sensation of running, I wasn't sure it was the sport that would take me far, and so I left it behind – for years. I pivoted towards other sports and activities. I tried table tennis, gymnastics, swimming, ballet and netball, to name a few. Outside of sports, I even tried the clarinet. Exploring all these activities helped me to see I was creative and curious. I learned I was good at some things and not others. It was my first understanding that sometimes you can give it your all and it may just not be suited to you – and that's okay.

Sports may not have been your thing when you were younger. You may have dismissed them entirely, decided they weren't for you – that's okay. Maybe PE felt more like punishment than play: being randomly selected for teams based on how popular you were; being made to do laps and laps of a field with no reason or intention given. For some millennials, sport brought only competition – with no space for creativity – purely judged on ability. And even when you tried your best, knowing you wouldn't be the best, the effort often went uncelebrated.

So why now? I need you to hear me when I say, our early choices don't have to define us for ever. Life has a way of circling back and offering second chances if you're open to them. When I was around ten, I made a significant decision to step away from running and explore other interests, and to allow myself to try new things. Yet, here I am now, fully embracing running again and loving it more than ever. That break from running wasn't the end of my journey – it was just a detour.

So, here is your reminder that, in life, you're not bound by the decisions you made as a kid, or even as a younger adult. You're allowed to pivot, to change direction, to go back and rediscover something you once set aside. If there's some-thing you gave up on in the past – whether it's a sport, a hobby or even a dream – don't be afraid to revisit it. You never know how it might fit in to your life now, or what kind of joy it might bring you. Sometimes the things we once walked away from end up being the things we're meant to return to. My relationship with running changed from a young child moving for the joy of it to running as a gateway for exploring other forms of movement.

While I know that PE was tricky for some, I was lucky. At secondary school, the PE department staff were so supportive; they made me feel seen for my sporting passion. These were women bold enough to work in a male-dominated profession, and I really looked up to them. They were mentors who not only celebrated my love for sport but actively discussed sports they excelled in and *how* they did it. These teachers were key in nurturing my love for sport when I was a teenager.

When I was a young girl, admitting you loved sport wasn't 'cool'. A lot of my peers would either forget their PE kits before a lesson or moan through every single second of the class. I was the polar opposite — a teacher's pet to the whole department. If they needed a last-minute sub for an away game, I'd always say yes. If the cupboard where the hockey sticks were kept was in disarray, I was the first to help tidy up. Every teacher encouraged my participation, whether in hockey, cricket, football or dance. Through their encouragement and constant support, they made me feel loved and wanted in the sporting space — something I know not many young girls experience. Their belief in me gave me a sense of belonging during a time when I was quietly battling questions of identity and acceptance. As a Black and mixed-race teenager in a school where 90 per cent of my classmates were white, I often felt the weight of being different. Racism is something I'll explore more deeply later in these pages, as it shaped how I saw myself. Because the truth is, alongside the usual turmoil of adolescence, I was also trying to make sense of where I fit in – or if I fit in at all.

One summer day in 2006, it was throws day: discus and shot put. I'd never tried them but had always been intrigued by throwing. In athletics, the track events are running-based, while field events comprise jumps and throws. Both the discus and shot put are throwing events. The discus is a circular metal plate, slightly larger than your hand, that the most elite athletes can launch over 70 metres. The shot put is a metal ball weighing 4 kilos for women or over 7 kilos for men; the best athletes in the world can throw it more than 20 metres.

When I picked up the discus, I had no idea if I could throw it at all. I remember the cold, metallic feel as I let the crease of my fingertips wrap round the edges. The discus fit perfectly in my hand, like a plug in a socket. As I listened to the technique cues from the teacher, I began the wind-up motion with my feet in a wind-staggered stance. Building momentum, rotating on my back foot and winding up with my arms, I had full control. As I rotated for the third and final time, I drove my hips like I was uncoiling a slingshot. The power transferred into the discus gliding from my fingertips, and off it soared. I watched the others' disci fall in front of them while mine was still flying through the air. When it landed, there were no other metal plates in sight. Mine had gone the furthest – over 20 metres. I punched the air with such power my shoulder almost left my body, pulled up into the sky. I had thrown it further than all of the boys! I felt so strong and free.

From that moment, I knew that this was my new life. After

this first throw, I joined the Brighton & Hove Athletics training nights and met the local throws coach, Bob. He took me under his wing, and every Tuesday and Thursday night through my teenage years, whether in torrential rain or blistering heat, I showed up. I gave it everything I had to give for little Emma, to help her live out her dream of going to the Olympics — something I could maybe achieve through throwing. Bursting out of my chest was the drive to be successful. I showed up to technical throws sessions, weight sessions and a never-ending number of throws. There is so much technique to learn when throwing, but I knew that if I kept showing up and putting in the work, I'd improve.

During this time, I barely ran, and I completely lost my love for it. I used to even complain about having to run 200m to warm up for throwing on training evenings. To be the best at throwing discus and shot, the most I needed to run were short, sharp, explosive sprints. Running stopped being something I did for fun or even competition. It had taken on a different meaning entirely: a means to improve in throwing but nothing more. That's not to say I didn't still find runners inspiring — as a spectator. I loved to watch races, whether of sprinters or long-distance runners. My eyes would widen when I saw them harness their raw power and speed in their races while looking so at ease. I admired them all, even more so now that I was training like an athlete and understood the work needed to compete at the highest level in sport. I didn't see running as something I could be 'successful' at during this time, so I didn't pursue it outside of throwing training. There was no notion that I could run just for the fun of running. My dream of competing and being the best in athletics had changed from aspiring to be like Kelly Holmes to wanting to achieve my Olympic goal through discus. So, I trained. A lot.

From thirteen to twenty-one, I competed to the highest level in the UK – everything from local county and southern women's leagues to county and national events. I won four county titles in both discus and shot put, achieved multiple podiums at southern county championships and performed well in the university leagues. Winning felt validating – that this sport I was putting my all into was actually reaping rewards, not just at a school level but on a bigger scale. But none of it would have happened if I hadn't just given it a go. When I was starting, my teacher told me to simply see what would happen if I just tried to throw. There was no pressure and no expectations. I did it to just *try*. Starting something new can be really hard. When I began throwing, I kept going because I was good at it, but also because I was curious about the intricacies of the technique and how I could learn it to the best of my abilities, throw further and continually improve. Is there a sport or a running distance you're intrigued to try? What's stopping you – the expectations of others, the possibility of failure? Remove all of that and let your curiosity win. Just start.

One of the national events I took part in was English Schools', where the best schoolchildren across all athletic disciplines were invited to compete against each other, representing their counties. It was like a mini-Olympics on a national scale – we even had an opening ceremony. I competed at this event on four consecutive occasions, and it was always the highlight of my year. As a young adult, being away with friends for a school trip and getting to compete in the sport you loved always felt magical. The venue and location changed yearly, and with my peers I would travel to the event after school on a Friday evening. Everyone from team Sussex (my team) met in the athletics stadium car park to board a coach. Kids chatted at a hundred miles an hour to their teammates about the weekend ahead, while parents anxiously checked the car to make sure all of the children's bags were collected. It was an honour to be selected, and being surrounded by the other talented athletes made you realize that even more so.

In my final year competing for Sussex, I made it through the qualifying round and came fifth out of twelve in the final – just before heading off to university. I was overjoyed to end on such a high, and as I returned to the team base I was met with high fives, fist bumps and big hugs from my teammates. I messaged my mum to tell her the news, and she instantly called me. This wasn't unusual. I assumed she was ringing to catch up or to congratulate me. I jumped to my feet as the phone rang and stepped off just outside the stalls to take the call. I was so chuffed with myself and eager to tell her everything. I rattled off every detail of the last hour, so excitedly I kept tripping over my own words. After my excitement wore off and I eventually paused for breath, Mum's tone changed from happy to concerned. Then, that line came:

'I need to tell you something.'

My dad had collapsed in the street and been rushed to hospital. He'd just come out of surgery. I felt sick. All the

13

excitement and joy of the last couple of days instantly disappeared. The cheering of those around me faded into a background blur as I stayed on the phone to my mum. I don't remember exactly how I felt after we hung up. When people spoke to me, I must have answered, chuckling or smiling back on autopilot. I remember watching my friends' races and events but not who won them. I remember the thunderous roar of the West Midlands team hollering their infamous chant — 'West Mids, best kids!' — but I wasn't really there. I was stuck inside my head. Every time I closed my eyes, my mind would conjure both the best- and worst-case scenarios about my dad. I got back on the coach to Brighton a muted version of myself, knowing life wouldn't be the same. I sat by the window, curled up in a tight ball, closed my eyes and prayed for none of it to be real.

The mind is such a powerful thing. I have absolutely no memory of what happened after I got off the coach. My mum tells me that we went to see my dad at the hospital, that at first I refused to go in, but eventually did. My brain has protected me from those emotions and the hurt I felt from seeing him in that hospital bed. It's something I've learned can happen with trauma.

My next real memory is from when my dad was out of the hospital recovering, when he told both my sister, Temi, and me what was wrong. We were in his flat, where we'd grown up, the place I knew as our home with him. Dad's flat was behind the smaller train station in central Brighton called London Road, and a set of half-cracked concrete steps led up to the entrance. The door was a striking emerald green with a gold knob in the middle. As it opened, I could smell our favourite mince and rice dish with boiled eggs. It was a staple meal that Dad always cooked for us – a classic family dish. A small wave of comfort came over me as the familiarity of something nostalgic and positive hit my nostrils, but that soon disappeared. The nineties pale-pink wallpaper brightened the room, but it didn't do anything for our mood. Dad knelt on the beige carpet to face us. There was no TV on or music playing like usual. I could hear my own heartbeat. He held our hands, and mine were clammy, my pulse almost punching out of my wrist. I tried to steady my breath. It didn't work. There was a sinking feeling in the pit of my stomach. I knew that whatever he was going to say next was going to change his life and ours for ever.

He told us he had a brain tumour known as a glioblastoma. It was stage 4 cancer.

My eyes let go of the tears, my body shaking with every sob. Dad held me and Temi on that floor in silence.

From then, my world crumbled. I knew that stage 4 cancer wasn't likely to be curable. I also knew that we wouldn't have much longer together. Living in the age of Google was both a blessing and a curse. I found every known paper, journal article and report of new exploratory research findings on Dad's condition to see if there could be a cure or a way to increase his life expectancy. But in 2011, and, sadly, even now, there was almost nothing that could be done. There were a few months left between finding out the news and me leaving for university, and during that time he declined rapidly. The Macmillan nurses, who are specialist cancer nurses, came to the flat daily during his last months to help his wife care for him. They were such a gift.

Cancer is so destructive. Initially, Dad lost his ability to speak and, along with that, his motor skills. I cannot tell you how soul-crushingly devastating it is to see the man you idolized as a dad — the man who would always put you first and care for you with the last penny he had — disappear in front of you. To know he couldn't answer the questions you've always wanted to ask. To speak to him and watch tears roll down his face and not be able to hear his thoughts or his feelings. To see him slowly lose the ability to eat. My dad was dying in front of my eyes, and so was my hope.

I haven't reflected on these memories until writing this, and they are just as raw now as they were then.

I left for university, heading to Brunel, just west of London. I created a small mountain of items to take with me on my bed, then stuffed them into bags. I read emails about Fresher's Fair over and over, planning which stalls I wanted to visit. I couldn't wait for the whole experience of leaving home, but it was tainted. I had to say goodbye, and I hate goodbyes. 2011 had already been full of them: to school friends, work colleagues and childhood besties, to venture off to university and go our separate ways. On my last day of school, my mum drove me in, with Classic FM, her favourite, on the radio. I was dressed in my leavers' shirt, and when Andrea Bocelli came on, singing 'Time to Say Goodbye', I started bawling and couldn't stop.

This goodbye was different. This wasn't just goodbye to 'pop to uni and be back at Christmas, no worries'. This was a goodbye with an unknown hanging over us. How long did Dad have left? Would I make it back to see him before the inevitable happened?

At university, I threw myself head first into all the activities, with netball and discus being my main loves. I knew this would help me cope, giving my mind a focus other than what was happening with Dad. I loved being part of a team, and the netball team became my new family. We had a mother-and-daughter ceremony, where you were adopted and welcomed in to the family lineage, which also ran through other teams on campus. As a cohort of people, all the sports teams felt like one big family at Brunel, and I came to rely on them as my support unit throughout my university life. Knowing that I had a family away from my 'real' family felt comforting, like I was really part of something special in the sports clubs.

University life helped to distract me, but there was always a layer of grief. If you have suffered the misfortune of seeing a loved one disappear in front of you, you will understand this feeling. You'd think that if someone you love was dying, you would want to be there all the time – but that wasn't the case for me. Part of me wanted to be there, to see my dad and support him. The other part of me wanted to protect the memories I held so dear of him before the illness. Grief is complex and contradictory sometimes, but whatever you feel, that is okay.

On 27 February, I got the call I'd been dreading. Dad was in the hospice at this point, and they believed he didn't have long left. It was time to go and say goodbye for the last time. I travelled down and sat by his bed, first with my mum and sister, and then alone. I needed to be there, but it hurt. It was like a slow, suffocating ache so deep in my chest it felt like it was consuming me, every breath I took feeling like a battle. The room was clinical and lifeless, like no part of our dad was there. I watched tears roll down my sister's face, with each tear rolled away a chance of him seeing us grow up, of him becoming a grandfather or walking us down the aisle. I held his cold hand and rested my head on it. I tried to hold my emotions in enough to speak and let him know that I'd always be his little girl, I'd always love him and strive to make him proud. There are words I shared with him that day I'll always keep close to my heart.

That night, I travelled straight back to university on the train. Being in the hospice any longer was much too painful. Though being around family should have helped, I just wanted to be back in my own world – away from the sadness, the hurt, the inevitable. When I arrived back at uni, it was late and I didn't know what to do with myself. I went to the twenty-four-hour library, sat in the corner and cried so many tears I wasn't sure I had any left. Then, my uni family showed up – some of my netball girls. Hannah, Adele and Sarah found me and took me back to their halls. They made me some food and tried to put the broken bits of glass that were me back together.

Two days later, on 29 February 2012, my dad, Tai, died. He was fifty-three. Nothing prepares you – even when you know it's coming.

In the months and years following his death, while I was at university, I can only describe it feeling like Dad was on holiday. I was in my 'Brunel bubble', where everything was safe and normal, like the outside world didn't exist, like Dad hadn't died – he just wasn't with me here. Staying at university while my dad was declining was one of the most difficult choices I've ever made, and it deeply shaped my grief after his death. I felt a constant tussle between two opposing forces: the guilt of not being there enough and the need to protect my own mental health. The guilt was overwhelming at times. I'd think about all the moments I missed: opportunities to see him, to visit my mum or to simply be there for my sister when she was struggling. I carried the weight of believing I had let them down, that I had somehow failed him during such a critical time. But even as I felt this guilt, I also understood that every visit, every glimpse of his decline, broke me a little more. Watching him fade was devastating, and I knew I couldn't withstand it more often than I did. It wasn't just about preserving my ability to keep going at university; it was about preserving my sense of self in the face of a heartbreak that I couldn't fully process at the time.

After his death, this inner conflict became a massive hurdle in my grieving process. I questioned my decisions constantly. Was I selfish for staying away? Should I have pushed myself harder to be there? Yet, at the same time, I had to come to terms with the reality that I had done what I could to survive an impossible situation. Finding peace with these opposing truths, guilt and self-preservation, has been a challenging and ongoing journey.

While at uni, I had my netball family, athletics team and lectures, which acted as a solid means of distraction. I focused in on them being my life. Sport felt like a safe space, a place where I knew joy would occur. I knew friends would be there, and I knew I could function without breaking down. I avoided going home to Brighton as it felt too painful, although I did miss my mum and sister. The pain was too raw, even to just think of Dad. It hurt that I knew I wouldn't see him walking down London Road Market like he used to. I wouldn't get to visit his flat to see him, or cycle with him round Preston Park. Brighton back then served as a reminder that my dad wasn't here any more.

But something new *was* here. Running. My first run back in Brighton after the funeral was to the outside of my dad's flat, with the emerald door. I ran through the park we used to cycle through as children, smelling the fresh coffee and bacon sandwiches at the cafe, while kids screamed at the top of their lungs and hurtled around the playground. I smiled to myself at the simplicity of it all. As I arrived at the street we grew up on, my heart dropped. The door wasn't emerald any more — it was red. A tear trickled down my face. It felt like another part of him had been taken away from me, with the painting of the door. On the run back to my mum's house, I remember deepening my breath. Calming my mind. Reminding myself of the control I had within me to weather this storm, the control I had to run and choose to move my body. That red door was a warning sign I hadn't realized I'd seen, pointing to the challenges I'd face in the years ahead.

You'll hear more about how running changed my life in the coming pages, but as I was growing up, as I tried to find out who I was and who I wanted to be, my relationship with running also evolved. From an innocent child who loved to run for the joy of it, and to release energy, to an older me discovering through adolescence what I wanted from life through the sports I took part in, the teams I became a part of, and the passion I found as I sought success in places beyond running. At some points, running wasn't even on my radar, but as you'll read, following my dad's illness and death, it became a pillar of my life to ground me during grief. I had an epiphany during this time: life is for living. More importantly, living in a way that brings you the most joy. Learning about myself and how I react to hard situations has shaped me as a person. As you'll find out, the journey towards myself was only just beginning.

FINDING YOUR WAY THROUGH

Grief is a journey that no one can truly prepare you for. Some days, it feels like you're standing at the bottom of a hill so steep it's impossible to even imagine reaching the top. The climb is relentless. Your legs scream, your breath is shallow and you constantly question whether you have the strength to continue. At times it demands everything from you: your heart, your body and the depths of your mind. But step by step, you move forwards.

This is something grief and running share. At its core, running is not about speed or grace – it's about persistence. You just need to keep going. On some days, grief is like the start of a long, uphill run. It feels impossible and as if there's no end in sight. On others, it's those long middle miles: days where nothing is outright painful, but the effort never lets up either. You're moving for what feels like for ever, but progress is slow. You're just putting one foot in front of the other, finding a rhythm and trying to keep going. But on some days, the sun is out, and you've found a downhill stretch. In these rare moments, gravity just takes over. The pressure eases, and for a brief time, there's relief. You remember how it feels to breathe deeply, to laugh, to feel free. Sometimes we can feel at one with our grief and able to bear it. But even those moments – depending on where you are in your journey – can be bittersweet, because they're fleeting and you know the next climb or bad day is lurking ahead.

People say that grief is the price we pay for love. I loved my dad, Tai, and even though we had limited time together, I want to tell you a little about him. I remember him as a man of few words, with the biggest heart, and as a person who was also the biggest kid. He loved a McDonald's and would join us in making the toys from the Happy Meals. I have the fondest of memories playing computer games together, specifically one named *Bejewelled*. In the early days of the internet, we'd play constantly to try and achieve an overall high score. I remember every evening for a whole month, Dad would play it, even after we'd gone to sleep, to try and reach first place. The next weekend, we arrived home to multiple boxes over-flowing with Rowntree's Fruit Pastilles. He had won them for us by getting the high score in his game! His huge grin, with eyes smiling, was everything. As much as this memory sticks with me because of the sweets, it also shows his intention and action. I saw that working hard towards something bore rewards. Sticking with sport and working hard would lead to success.

Running was something my parents championed. If events fell on my weekends with my dad, he drove me here, there and everywhere. He always, along with Mum, supported my love of sport from an early age, on occasion even taking part themselves. One memory I'll cherish for ever is my dad running in the father's Sports Day race. He started the race, lining up with the other dads in their jeans and chinos, all of them searching for the feeling of glory from their youth. They took their marks, trying to be nonchalant about the race but secretly eyeing each other up. The gun was raised, and *bang*, off they went. Dad was speedy out of the gates until, halfway down the field, his hamstring pulled – and with it, took away victory. He left the track with a laughing wince and a smile, and I felt his participation as a reflection of the love he felt for me, by taking part in something that meant so much. I loved witnessing his courage to try. These memories of Dad will always stay with me, and I can't help but wish we had more time together. I don't believe anyone who has lost someone doesn't think this.

Dad also enjoyed cycling and, in the summer, we would cycle around the park. When winter came, we would go bowling or swimming instead. He was adamant that my sister and I would both know how to swim and encouraged us to practise with him outside the lessons we took, even if I'm not the best at it now. When the Olympics were on, he would always have it playing in the background, and we'd discuss my Olympic dream and the dedication required to get there.

I had a deep love for my dad, but it also came with a drop of angst from his parenting style. There were rules in place for our safety and care, but sometimes they seemed so strict that I felt like pushing them. If I ever pushed a boundary, my dad would look me in the eyes sternly and in his deep voice say: 'Do you want to find out?' The answer was always: absolutely not. Through my young teenage years, I communicated this with a shuffle of my feet and, without making eye contact, uttered 'no' before huffing and puffing myself into silence. Anger wasn't something I ever showed to my dad because, well, I didn't want to find out his reaction. Now, I wish I'd got over it quicker, broken the silence, hugged him and apologized. That constant awareness of limits, consequences and self-control, in one sense, laid the foundation for the discipline I now carry into my own training. Running requires a similar respect for boundaries. You learn when to push and when to pull back, when to listen to the voice telling you to keep going and when to yield to the one warning you not to overstep.

I didn't know it then, but all those huffed silences and withheld teenage protests were training in self-restraint and endurance. My dad's voice still echoes in the background — not as fear now, but as structure, as steadiness. It taught me that consistency matters, that showing up even when you don't feel like it builds something stronger.

My first true memories of life with Dad are from my school days. The summer fêtes at primary school were a highlight of my childhood. The local school playing field was adorned with multicoloured flags and multicoloured bunting strung across the trees, the smells of hot dogs and burgers filling the air and a path of stalls with gazebos lining the field with every type of bright, enticing entertainment a young child could desire. There was face painting, bouncy castles, bean bag throwing, hook-a-duck, bric-a-brac stalls, cake stalls and, of course, the stage, where the children performed their group summer dance. My parents were the king and queen of the barbecue most years. Having both had culinary backgrounds, they knew exactly what they were doing. Some of my happiest moments were seeing them there, working and laughing together. I could really see how they worked as a team and came together to support not only my schooling life, but me.

When thinking about my battle with grief, I wonder why we aren't taught about death as children – at school, about the emotions, the pain and the sadness it brings. It's something we all will experience in our lifetime, yet there's no standard curriculum, education or guidance on how to manage, navigate or cope with it – especially as a child.

I first came across this when I was seven. I was taken out of a lesson by an assistant teacher and told my auntie Elizabeth had died after fighting leukaemia. My auntie was an incredible woman – she began her career as a nurse, firstly in the RAF (Royal Air Force), and in later life devoted her work to helping and saving premature babies. I'll never forget a photo my mum has of her holding a tiny baby in her care, just the size of one of her hands. She and my mum were very close. They had dreamed of growing old together and would often chat and plan what they'd do in later life.

I didn't go to the funeral up north; I didn't want to. The thought of being somewhere so sad, seeing my mum hurt and upset wasn't something I could handle. Even now, as an adult, seeing her crying or in pain is difficult for me. Seeing her vulnerability – her 'inner child'– reminds me that we are all just living this life for the first time. Pain affects everyone, and death comes for us all. As a child, this was very difficult for me to understand. I knew my aunt was gone and that I'd never see her again. I knew my mum was in a lot of pain, and

I saw that the pain didn't go away after the day of the memorial had passed. I didn't really understand it all at seven, but I'd have to learn to, and twelve years later, I *had* to go to the funeral — this time my father's.

There were three key things that helped me take control of my emotions and find who I was again while I was in the depths of grief: speaking to people, community and, eventually, running. The people in my life, other than my mum, from whom I could seek support were my netball coaches Camilla and Tee. At university, I was in a bubble where the outside world didn't seem like it was happening. My family seemed so far away, and I didn't want to worry them. Both Camilla and Tee actively gave me permission to lean on them. Meeting them before netball training sessions to talk and explain how I was feeling allowed me to validate my own emotions. They not only gave empathy but also didn't treat me any differently from anyone else in training and matches. Whether I was angry, upset, overwhelmed or frustrated, Camilla and Tee made me feel heard. Their selfless acts taught me a lot about being a coach and what the role embodies. Coaching isn't just about showing up and delivering a session; it's about the difference you can make to others with your time, empathy and support.

My 'netball family' was also there for me, but although it wasn't true, I felt like a burden to my peers. Being 'broken' was all-encompassing. I'd wake up and have to force myself to get through the day when all I wanted was to stay inside. Resilience to persevere was key. I wanted to be the 'normal' nineteen-year-old Emma around my friends, not the one struggling to get out of bed through sadness to come and train.

Right in the middle of this difficult time, I was lucky enough to take part in a once-in-a-lifetime experience that has done more than perhaps anything else to cement the incredible power of sport and community in most people's eyes. I was accepted as a Games Maker, a volunteer for the London 2012 Olympics. Volunteering at both Wimbledon and the Olympic Stadium was the best experience, a welcome distraction from my grief. I was living my childhood dream of being at an Olympics, even if it wasn't how I'd initially imagined it. I met young and old sports fanatics like me from all around the world, and as a collective, there was heartwarming pride that we were helping to host the Games. I felt part of something, I felt welcome, and I felt honoured to be there – positive feelings that I hadn't experienced for a while.

I started my days early, up at 2 or 3 a.m. catching the night bus, and then jumped on the fast train to the stadium in Stratford to start my shifts at 4 a.m. Every morning, hurried footsteps would shuffle off the train, carrying laughter from the other volunteers – not something you'd usually hear that early in the morning. We collected our badges and breakfasts and would find out where we were going to be for the day. During my time at the stadium, the Paralympics were on. I remember it being one of the first times I had seen blade runners in person. These blades were used by those with lower-limb amputations. They attach to the remaining limb(s) to allow the athletes to propel forwards and run majestically. Their ability to adapt and be so brilliant at running was incredible. It

29

reminded me of the power that running has to keep people moving forwards. At Wimbledon for the Olympics, I was fortunate enough to meet players, experience some of the matches and see Andy Murray win *that* gold medal. From sitting at home yearly, watching fans bustle around Wimbledon, it was an incredible honour to walk the halls as a staff member, seeing it all through my Games-Maker lens. Tucked behind Centre Court was where our daily meetings took place, discussing the previous day's events and our allocated stations for the day. People of all ages worked, collaborated and represented the Olympic volunteers passionately. That summer of joy was what I needed. It reminded me of why I did the sports I did. It reminded me of the power of sport to shift a city and a nation to support one another.

In my second and third years of university, I threw myself into training and working for my degree, instead of actually processing my grief. Even when advised by supervisors and my mum to go, I actively declined therapy. Back then, I saw it as a weakness, and also as pointless. Why would I talk to a total stranger who didn't know me or how I felt, when I couldn't even figure my emotions out myself? I graduated from Brunel University with a Bachelor of Science in Sport with a 2:1 and I was elated, considering that these had been the hardest years of my life. I moved in to shared accommodation – a room a woman let out in her house.

I started working full time for Nike at their flagship store on Oxford Street after graduating. I had dreamed of working for this brand and loved the idea of growing within the company. I knew all the Nike-sponsored athletes, whether in running, tennis or basketball. I knew the latest model names and numbers and how they all slightly differed, even before I'd taken the staff training. The people I worked with were some of the funniest, kindest and most caring humans. I'd be on a lunch break, and someone would walk over to check how I was doing. On the shop floor, someone would spot me having a challenging interaction with a customer and stand next to me for support. The support I felt from these colleagues was so impactful as my mind began to release the grief I had suppressed for so long. While working at Nike, I was able to show up to work, put on my customer-facing act and smile as if everything was okay. But as soon as I had a day off, my grief would hit.

I spent any time I wasn't working alone in my room watching TV, riding the rollercoaster of emotions in my head. I had a mini fridge at the foot of my bed – a little square one that could only fit the essentials: for me then, milk. My daily diet for many of those days at home was three bowls of cereal. As a twenty-something on a low salary, it was economical, but the major reason for my cereal diet was that it required little to no effort whatsoever. I couldn't bring myself to make real, tasty, nutritious food because I was numb. Some days I didn't even go downstairs to wash the bowl from the meal earlier in the day. I'd reuse it for breakfast, lunch and dinner. Very little effort was required other than shuffling to the edge of my bed, opening the fridge, pouring in the cereal and milk, and food was served. I didn't think, or care, about the nutritional value of what I consumed. I was proud of myself for eating, but I couldn't do more than that.

Social media was also having an impact on how I was feeling back then. Ever since I began engaging in media and social channels in the early 2000s, the narrative of the 'ideal' body type has been very Eurocentric. Namely, skinny, white, petite and without an ounce of fat. By 2014, there was a changing narrative that being strong was better than being skinny – or at least that's what I saw on the internet. I took selfies during that time and remember thinking that abs would help to make me happy in this moment. I was battling my mind to find positives and reasons to be happy; I thought if I had abs and a better self-image, I'd feel better – be better. My mind swirled with thoughts like: *If I look good and people validate it, then I'll be happy.* I convinced myself that having abs was the answer, rather than eating better, going outside or even speaking to someone about my emotions. I became someone who ate the bare minimum while going to the gym. I wasn't starving myself, but I tried to eat less to chase these abs that I thought were a ticket to feeling good. I was trying to cling on to anything to find hope. I was lying to my mum as well, keeping her in the dark as to how much I was struggling. I wanted to protect her from seeing her daughter in pain. As someone who had always been pretty independent, I was adamant I would figure this out myself.

I felt alone, yet I was surrounded by people. I was deeply unhappy, yet able to put on an act and be bubbly in situations where I had to. I felt like a lost child, but society saw me as an adult who was supposed to know how to look after myself.

I was scared of asking for help, and what that might look like. Grief had me in a chokehold. Unsure of my next steps, I took them — literally. I finally realized I had to do *something*, and it turned out that running became the catalyst for a much bigger change in my mental health. While there had been a little running in my teenage discus training and uni netball warm-ups, it had been a long time since I'd even considered running just to run. But one morning in September 2014, I decided it was time. I woke up as usual, heavy with the sadness I felt each day, but I was sick of it. I just didn't want to feel it any more. I sat up in bed and swung my feet to the cold, hard wooden floor. It was never warm, but that day I flinched as I placed my feet down. I took a deep sigh, and as I turned my head to the door, I saw my brand-new work trainers (Nike Pegasus) laced and ready to go by the side of the bedpost. I loved new shoe day. When we received uniforms every quarter, we were allowed to pick our shoes for that season. The previous day at work, we'd received our running kit as part of our uniform, and these new clothes were also on my bedroom floor. As I stumbled to the bathroom, I looked out of the window and saw the day was dry, with the sun bursting free from behind a swathe of grey clouds that had covered the sky the last two days. Maybe this was a sign, I thought. Maybe today didn't have to be filled with gloom about Dad not being here. Maybe I could change this day to have hope.

I got into my new kit, laced up my new shoes, opened the Nike Running app on my phone and headed out the door. As soon as the chill hit my face, I worried it was too cold to run and began questioning my choices. Only five seconds later, a new, optimistic voice overpowered my doubts with a simple:

You can do this. The first step felt like exhaling after holding your breath for too long. I felt the ground beneath my feet, pushing me up and on to my next step as I searched for the right rhythm, I was doing it – I was running. For the first kilometre, I couldn't find my breath. I dodged crumbled leaves and dog poo on the road, trying not to get my new shoes dirty. I fought to keep control of my lungs. *Maybe I couldn't do this*.

At the time, I was living in Mitcham, a little town about 8 miles south of central London. There were so many green spaces for me to explore. As I headed towards the local park, a woman in the allotments smiled at me as I ran past. I smiled back. *Was this real joy I felt?* With every step, the emotional load I was carrying became lighter and lighter. Once I reached the park, I thought: *just one lap.* I had clearly forgotten my competitive streak. As I eased in to lap one, that soon became two and then, three laps. That day I ran 5.1km. When I stopped my watch, I took a deep breath and smiled as tears began to roll down my face. I'd found the release I'd craved. Like water breaking through a dam, finally allowed to flow freely.

And running wasn't *just* running. My science brain also knew that if I'd run, I'd need to fuel that effort. I had to eat – and eat well – if I wanted to do this. I'd have to shower after running because I'd be sweaty, which meant putting on clean clothes and taking care of myself. It was all quite primitive: woman must eat if she runs, woman must wash if she runs.

On my way home, I bought ingredients for a chicken stir-fry for dinner. When I got in, I showered, dressed and ate a substantial meal. That simple step of one foot in front of the other led me to all these other steps of self-care. That run changed the course of my life. You never know how a single step – how taking a chance on something – can change you for the better. That one step led me to thousands more, and with each step, I came back to myself a little more.

Running became a regular part of my life during this time, and gradually, I spent less time in my room. My mini fridge now held more than just milk. I saw my friends more. Little by little, I ran further, pushed myself a little harder. I went on that run to my dad's door in Brighton and used this time of moving my body to let grief wash over me. On these runs, I felt free, and as the sun hit my face during another lap of the park, I found flickers of joy I'd thought I might never feel again.

These early runs were just the beginning. I began to set myself challenges – the first to commemorate my dad's death, raising money for a brain tumour charity in the lead-up to his birthday. For twenty days, I ran 5km, rowed 5km and cycled 5km. These daily 5km runs felt like the first real runs of my life. During these runs, I ran with intention, with purpose – not just to develop myself but to help others facing the same battles as Dad. This challenge felt like the birth of a new me – a me who had re-found her childlike drive and energy and channelled it into running, a me who had found a reason to get up and better herself. It was the start of a beautiful journey. I completed the challenge and found new meaning in exercise and running.

Please know, I didn't run a full 5km every time I went for a run in my early days. I was not 'fast' every day. I didn't feel great every day. I ran for the feeling after the run. The feeling of letting go. The act of running felt like I got to escape my problems for a while and quiet my mind. I sometimes ran to improve my times, but the destination was rarely the goal for me.

I need you to know that every run you do is valid. If you walk in your run, even for large parts of it, it's still a run. Whatever distance you cover, however 'slow' your pace, your run is still worthy and an incredible achievement. If you run 5km in twenty minutes or you run it in forty minutes or longer, you've still run 5km. Speed is arbitrary. I say this because, despite the running community being a positive and welcoming space, there can sometimes be a sense of comparison or competition. People can judge the paces other runners share on social media or in person. I've heard conversations mocking those who aren't 'fast enough' to enter races or meet cut-off times. Recently, there was a huge debate online about the validity of 'slower' runners entering world-renowned marathons such as Boston and Tokyo and making the cut-off times. Eliud Kipchoge, a legend in the running space and arguably the greatest marathon runner of all time, is a huge advocate for inclusivity in running. In one TV interview, I remember him saying that you don't have to be the fastest runner in the world, just the fastest runner that YOU can be.

Speed is irrelevant. Kipchoge is one of the fastest runners of all time, but he still holds space and admiration for *every* runner. When he was interviewed about his support for a six-hour marathon runner, he professed that he could never imagine himself running for six hours and that those who do inspire him. One of the greatest distance runners of all time is inspired by *you*. Everyone in the running space is welcome. The only battle — if any — is the one against the version of you that showed up last.

As I continued to run, I decided to document my journey on social media. In those early days, I didn't post with any kind of plan. But as I posted, I ended up stumbling across a community — one of runners and fitness people who simply wanted to build each other up, leaving comments and direct messages of support to one another from all over the world. My confidence as a runner grew, and I was brave enough to sign up for a 10k later that year. Slowly, I began to find myself again. Running on both good days and hard days strengthened my mind to tackle whatever life threw at me, and I began to stop running away from myself and instead ran towards the newer version of me. One where grief didn't control my choices.

Grief isn't a journey with a clear end-point. The hard emotions don't disappear, because your love for the person you lost will never go, and you'll always hold that love — and those feelings — with you. What grief does do is shift. It evolves, and it becomes something you learn to carry and accept. Bad runs, like bad days, still show up. Sometimes they catch you off guard, and this still happens to me.

A few weeks ago, I was running in my local park and 'Dance with My Father' by the legendary Luther Vandross came on shuffle. It's a beautiful song, and I started singing along to it as I ran. Before I knew it, tears were streaming from my eyes. I stopped, wiped them away and smiled. The smile was an acknowledgement that yes, I still carry the grief, yes, I still

37

miss my dad deeply – but the weighted vest of emotion I wear gets a little lighter the more years that go on. I know I'll never take that vest off, but it will continue to lighten.

I've learned that running can, and has, become a vehicle to help me overcome the hardships and mental instability I have and will continue to experience. It's now my default to still show up for a run even in my cloudiest, foggiest times, because I know that giving myself time to simply *be* in the run brings me back to myself. The movement will always have that power over me, no matter how far I go. You will go through struggles in your life – big emotions, hard challenges that you don't know how to talk about or untangle, or even feel. If you'd like one bit of advice, one act that helped me more than anything I've ever done, take one step. One step is all you have to do. If it leads to more, amazing! If it spills out into other areas of your life and ignites change, incredible. If not, that's also okay. But even the act of choosing to take one step, choosing yourself, is a power and a strength you hold that no one can take away.

FINDING CHANGE

The first things that people see when they look at me are that I'm a woman, I'm Black, with brown skin, and I have an Afro. The order in which they notice may vary, but these are simple facts that people perceive, subconsciously or consciously, when they look at me. I grew up understanding that my hair and the colour of my skin were viewed through many differing lenses – sometimes admired and seen as beautiful, but in many ways policed, exoticized, dismissed and even ridiculed. This noticeable conflict within society greatly impacted how palatable I thought I was, not just to my surroundings but the world at large.

As we dive in to race and its many layers, know that this chapter will twist and turn in all sorts of directions. If you're reading this as a person of colour, I want to highlight that I'm going to discuss my experiences of racism. If it feels like too much or brings up traumatic moments in your life, protect your peace and feel free to skip, or engage however works for you. Running is still at the forefront of the chapter, but I'm also going to look at some of the complex, intertwined layers of my identity, which can feed in to *why* we run.

To do that fully, we need to look at the society we live in.

I grew up in what I believed until recently was a very diverse city. Brighton is a welcoming seaside town with the hustle and bustle of a bigger city like London at its core. It's well known for its large community of LGBTQ+ inhabitants, and it was because of this that I assumed it was completely diverse. But from a racial perspective, that is certainly not the case. The 2021 census of Brighton and Hove recorded 85.4 per cent of the population as white and only 4.8 per cent identified as mixed race like me.[1] For context, the UK average is 83 per cent white but only 2.7 per cent mixed race. [2] As a mixed-race person in Brighton – and even the UK – I guess I'm pretty unique in that sense.

My mum is British and was born and raised in Grimsby, northern England, and my dad was Nigerian, born and raised in Lagos, West Africa. They met in 1987, married and had me in 1992. During the eighties and nineties in the UK, mixed-race couples were still frowned upon. I remember my mum sharing stories of the racist encounters she and Dad experienced when they were dating – such as the time they were harassed by a group of white men as they walked past her old workplace. As the men approached, my mum crossed the road to avoid them. My dad searched to see if there was anything around him that he could use to protect them in case of attack. Luckily it wasn't needed in the end and the men scurried off to the next pub, but the fact that my parents needed to make these split-second choices to protect themselves simply for existing together is bleak.

My mother and father were only the second generation of

white and Black people to commonly have children together. She speaks of how 'friends' of hers didn't attend the wedding because she was marrying a Black man. One reason for these attitudes is embedded in the UK's historical makeup – the systemic racism that lives and breathes in the UK now, and always has. If I *really* went into it, we'd need a whole other book, but I'll do my best to summarize in this first historical turn of the chapter.

The Transatlantic Slave Trade began in the 16th century and continued for hundreds of years. Black men, women and children were held in unimaginable conditions, taken from their homelands, dehumanized and commodified by European countries. During this time, slave ships would be filled with people at African ports, then sailed to the USA and UK. The most notable trade hubs were along the West African coast, including present-day Nigeria, Benin, Cameroon, Ghana and Togo. Trade also extended to regions in East and Southern Africa, such as Tanzania and Mozambique. Cities in the UK like Cardiff, Bristol and especially Liverpool sent goods such as textiles, alcohol and firearms to West Africa. These goods, along with money, were exchanged for enslaved people who were taken to the USA and sold, and then ships returned to Liverpool full of goods like sugar, tobacco and cotton. This was known as the triangular trade route.[3] Slavery was abolished in the British Empire, but societal ideas and beliefs about Black people were still very negative. A mixed couple, even in the 1900s, was still highly frowned upon. Many people believed that Black people were an inferior race to white people. This belief was underpinned by the theory of

41

eugenics, a concept coined by Sir Francis Galton in 1883, which means 'good breeding'. Galton promoted the idea of *positive eugenics* – encouraging those deemed 'fit' to have larger families. However, this theory was soon distorted by others into *negative eugenics*, aimed at limiting the reproduction of those considered 'unfit'. As a result, the idea of racial mixing was viewed by many at the time as dangerous and unacceptable.

In 1930, a report was published that was not only deeply racist but also has been completely debunked. Anthropologists Rachel M. Fleming and Muriel Fletcher researched what they termed 'hybrid children' in their work titled the 'Fletcher Report' (also known as the 'Colour Problem in Liverpool and other ports').[4] The research, conducted in Liverpool, was used to try and define Liverpool's 'half-castes' as a problem and blight to the 'British way of life' in the city. The work and its claims were highly controversial. Fleming and Fletcher stated that mixed-race children were likely to be more sickly because of the genes inherited from their Black fathers, that they would have below-average intelligence and that as adults they would struggle for work, face discrimination and have little to no future. Fletcher frequently used the phrase 'handicapped by their colour' in her research, linking the ideas that Black and white races mixing in Britain in the early 1900s was a problem and that being mixed race was a 'handicap'. The UK played a huge part in slavery, colonialism and imperialism – all of which continue to shape policies which we have today. A crazy example of a policy that has only recently ended, is that until 2015, UK taxpayers' money was still going to ex-slave owners to recompense them for the loss of income once the slave trade was abolished.[5] Yes, you read that right – until 2015. Systemic racial bias runs deep, even to this day.

My mum guided and supported me as I grew up, answering questions about my mixed identity and about the colour of my skin. Throughout the seventies and eighties, she dated people of various of races and was very attuned to the racial discrimination and hardships suffered by people of colour. With me as her daughter, she did her utmost to bring me to spaces where I was seen. Growing up, I always knew I was different. I was darker-skinned than all of my white peers; I had a bigger nose; I was taller and consequently always looked older. Most of my friends until I was around eleven were blonde- or brown-haired and blue-eyed. It was all I knew, other than my dad, sister, extended family and aunties from the African side of my family.

Some of my first memories are of visiting supermarkets with my mum, which I adored – a place with all my favourite foods to buy and explore, to find the latest toy or video (yes, it was the nineties). The vastness of the supermarket was exciting. I know my mum thought otherwise. On occasion, she would go to customer services having 'lost' me as I'd snuck away mid-shop to go to the bakery or to the pick 'n' mix aisle to eye up the chocolate raisins. The tannoy would ring out: 'Customer call. Emma Kirk-Odunubi, your mum is at customer service waiting for you. Please come here to find her.'

For our supermarket visits, I'd rock up with the Lamborghini of kiddies' shopping trolleys: a car with a yellow basket, green wheels and a red handlebar, all made of shiny plastic.

43

I'd come dressed just as colourfully, pushing the car trolley with my handwritten shopping list. But it was during some of these trips, when my Afro was growing out, that I remember the staring. I can't have been older than five or six, and I remember seeing other children looking dumbfounded at me. Some had shock on their faces, and some would stop in their tracks to gawk at me. On one trip, a young boy yelled at his mum, 'Look, she's got hair like a monster!'. I blinked once slowly, then again, trying to process what had just happened, my face frozen. I ran back to my mum. Now that I'm older, I've come to realize the effect those words had on me. At five years old, I learned that my hair was scary, a problem. From around this age, my Afro became something I grew to hate. This hate was reaffirmed by the bullying.

At six, I was playing in the playground of my primary school. The playground was split into two, one half decorated with wooden flower boxes full of red and pink geraniums. In the right-hand corner was a beautiful wooden Wendy house that was always popular to play in. The second half of the playground contained the netball and football pitches, marked out by multicoloured lines. Usually, the older years stayed on the pitches while the younger years played in the bottom half of the playground.

One day, I was playing with my friends in the Wendy house and we decided to play tag – a game where you chase people around the playground and one person is 'it'. If you get tapped, you then become 'it' and do the chasing (an elite childhood game). Some of the older boys were playing that day too, and I loved this, as my fast little running legs could occasionally

44

outrun them. As I zigzagged away, I'd smirk and clap for myself in celebration. There was a boy, let's call him Cam (although that is not his real name), who was 'it' during the last five minutes of the game. Cam had the wildest, curly locks of ginger hair and had already hit his growth spurt, towering above many of us. I sprinted round the corner of one of the flower boxes as he tagged me, but it felt different. He *grabbed* me instead and pulled me over to the fence. Grabbing my hair, he wrapped it round the fence. Round and round he went, creating one almighty knot. I didn't even try to move. I knew I was stuck. Initially, my friends laughed, but then my close friends went to get me help. As tears trickled down my face and I wrapped my arms around one of my friends, a teacher came to my aid. The knots Cam had made were so bad that they had to use a pair of classroom scissors to detach me from the fence. I sobbed for most of the day. All I knew was this: my hair was different, I had been bullied for that difference, and therefore, I hated my hair.

For the rest of my childhood, I did anything and everything I could to avoid having my hair stand out. My dad, who I saw at this point every other weekend since my parents' divorce when I was four, didn't know about the struggles I had with my hair. It wasn't something I believed he could understand or empathize with, so I stayed silent about it with him by choice. But with my mum, I used to cry, wishing I had straight blonde hair like my friends. The ultimate goal as a child was to grow my hair long enough that I could put it in a bun or in braids and have it in a 'normal' and 'pretty' style. Having my hair in braids was the only time I remember getting compliments on my hair from those outside my family. It was more appealing, and I looked more beautiful in braids, according to societal norms. The braids made me feel more accepted, even if they did end up hurting a lot and damaging my scalp (a sign they were too tight). I felt prettier and, from a running perspective, I looked like the runners I aspired to be. If that was how they had their hair to run fast, well then so could I. In reality, no one around me looked like me with my hair braided or not. But at least in braids I was classed as pretty, right?

While I didn't face everyday violence, I grew up with a deep sense of not being the 'ideal', especially through secondary school. During puberty, particularly, my hormones were running around with overwhelming crushes and emotions. As everything changed, so did my self-confidence and worth, as I figured out who I was in the world. With that, I was hyper-aware I wasn't the blonde-haired, blue-eyed girl all the boys found attractive. I didn't fit that mould. I wanted to be liked, to join in the banter and make friends. My secondary school was huge and there was some diversity, but I could still only count the number of Black people in my year on my hands. It was the first space where I began to learn the hardship of having my skin colour and most regrettably, had the realization that if you can't beat them, you accept defeat and self-deprecate. And that I did.

When learning the small amount of Black history that we did study, we watched the series *Roots*. It wasn't about Black joy but about slavery, *of course*. The series is the story of a man, Kunta Kinte, who is taken from his African village and enslaved in the US. While we were watching, a boy in my form turned and said to me in a Nigerian accent, 'Eh, Kunta Kinte, go back to the ship'. Being a teenager and wanting to keep the peace and stay friends with everyone, I laughed it off and said nothing. For weeks, the boy would call me that name at any given moment. A teacher pulled him up on it and I told her it was a joke and to leave it be. Did it hurt deep down? Of course. Did he do it to the one other Black boy in the class? No – because he was popular. I had to laugh it off because it was easier. Easier than me addressing the situation. Easier than me making a fuss. Yes, he was calling me the name of a slave, but it was easier to allow it to happen and quieten my feelings in order to 'fit in'. My confidence as a teen was lacking, but confidence in my ability to do sport? I had that. Participating in sport and athletics was where I found my confidence. My lack of self-belief and self-worth as a person, when I wasn't in an athletic situation, made me feel like a lost girl sometimes.

But the power that sport brought to my worth, shaping me and my identity, was one of the things that helped me accept the skin I was in. Here was one of the first true moments where sport became more than just something I was good at – it became my escape. When everything else felt uncertain, sport gave me structure. When I didn't have the words for what I was feeling, movement gave me a way to release it and bring joy back to me. Training sessions, competitions, even the quiet rhythm of performing discus drills gave my mind somewhere to go when it felt overwhelmed. I didn't have to explain myself when I was moving. I just had to show up, perform and enjoy myself.

At university, I'm lucky in that I don't remember experiencing any overt racism. My university was extremely diverse, but even in that environment, I still wrestled with feelings of 'not belonging', even to the race I felt I had belonged to in the past. This was nothing to do with the people I was around – it was more about what I'd been conditioned to feel. During my time there, I felt that I couldn't join the ACS (Afro-Caribbean Society), as I didn't feel Black enough to be a part of it. I look back now, feeling sorry for my younger self, who didn't feel confident to lean in to who I was – the part of me that is Black. As I grew up, the white part of me was easy to learn and understand, as it was embedded in British culture, taught through history, and I was surrounded daily by people who were white. Being Black, for me, was something I knew was part of who I was, but back then, I didn't know how to lean in to it, learn more about it or feel confident in doing so.

Spending time with my dad, especially during those awkward teenage years, I didn't want to ask him questions about our Blackness or interact much at all – something I regret now.

There's a complexity in holding both identities – two cultures, two histories, sometimes in conflict, sometimes in harmony, and learning to live with the tension of that. If I lean too much in to my Blackness, am I denying my mother's heritage? But in the same breath, knowing I physically present to the world as Black, I should lean in to that. Over time, I've come to see that being mixed isn't about confusion – it's about complexity. It's not about not belonging anywhere – it's about learning to belong deeply to yourself.

I recently listened to a phenomenal podcast called *Mixed Up* where two mixed-race women, Nicole and Emma, share their own experiences and nuances of growing up mixed race. They shared one of the best identity descriptions I'd ever heard: 'I'm Black and mixed race.' It was like someone had fitted the missing part of the puzzle to how I feel. *I'm Black and mixed race.*

In my mid-twenties, the day after the UK decided to vote for Brexit, I was on a run in South London. A white couple walked past me and said, 'Go back to the jungle!'

I'll never forget it. I almost stopped to ask them if they were talking to me (they most definitely were). I felt disrespected. Shocked. Like I'd been hit with an imaginary slap that left no mark, but that had a sting that lingered. I was also relieved because I was running at that moment. Running that day helped me stay safe. Not only did it literally take me away from racism, but it also gave me a space to remember who I was and push back against their view of disgust.

At thirty years old, I know I'm mixed race, but I'm also Black. My own feelings are that I'm not seen as white enough to be white but also not Black enough to be Black. It's a weird mix of having felt inferior in some Black spaces because of my own lack of confidence, and also being acutely aware when I'm the only one who looks like me in white spaces – and of the microaggressions that go unnoticed by 99 per cent of those people in those places. Microaggressions are those subtle, often unintentional comments or actions that reveal bias or stereotypes – usually without the person even realizing it. They're small moments that have a big impact. I can't tell you the number of times my surname has been either butchered (likely through fear of saying it wrong and then actually doing so), or one of my 'favourite' memories: the assistant judge at a discus competition asking if we could just call me Emma Kirk because it was easier. *Sigh*. In the last ten years of working in the world of social media, influencing and events, situations like these have been the norm. I've also felt when I've been the token invite and questioned whether I was actually worthy of being in the room or if I was there simply to tick a box for a brand's marketing team. It's a very challenging situation to be in.

Growing up, I learned to straddle these two differing worlds, and after some processing of my own, I realized that I was so able to adapt to both of these worlds that I hadn't noticed I didn't belong to either. I'll be honest with you: even to this day, I struggle with my identity. As I've matured into a young woman, it has been hard, and writing this book has been the catalyst for me to have difficult conversations and look inwards. I don't know my true self because I've tried to please both sides of society and not focused on the one thing that counts above all else: myself and who I believe I am – who I want to be.

Colourism is an ever-present reality, and I recognize that, as a lighter-skinned Black person, I'm often seen more favourably in the world we live in. Colourism is bias or discrimination based on how light or dark someone's skin tone is – *within* the same racial or ethnic group. It's that unspoken preference for lighter skin that shows up in everything from beauty standards to job opportunities. So while racism is about race, colourism is more about shade. I understand that those with darker skin than mine face a deeper level of discrimination – more scrutiny, more systemic bias and more overt forms of racism. I'll never fully know what that feels like, and I don't pretend to. All lived experiences of racism are valid and abhorrent. But I acknowledge the privilege that proximity to whiteness gives me, even if it's marginal. And if that means my voice is heard a little louder in certain rooms, then I'm going to use it! Not to speak *over* others, but to *amplify* what needs to be said. I don't want to be palatable. I want to be purposeful.

The internal divisions that colourism creates within our communities serve only to weaken us. There should be no 'them' and 'us' within a marginalized group. Our fight isn't against each other – it's alongside one another. We can't even attempt to dismantle racism without also dismantling the hierarchy that exists within our own identities. Solidarity means making space, listening with humility, and recognizing when to speak and when to step back. If I can be part of that shift, then I'll keep showing up, loudly and intentionally.

The Olympics meant a lot to me as a child and still do to this day. When I reflect on why I was and am so captivated by them, representation sticks at the forefront of my mind. At the Olympics, Black people are championed for their ability; it's a place where we're celebrated. Historically, for many Black people, it's been a way of proving our worth on the world stage. One of the athletic greats, Jesse Owens, put up a silent middle finger to the Nazi German regime when he won his four gold medals in 1936. It completely went against the 'pure

51

white race' ideals Hitler strived for. The Black Power Salute in 1968 by Tommie Smith and John Carlos was done to protest the discrimination and social injustice faced by Black people in the US. Smith raised his right fist to represent Black power, while Carlos raised his left to represent Black unity. This move sparked mixed feelings from the US team and subsequently had them banned from the athletes' village. Also on the podium was Peter Norman, a white Australian sprinter who came second in the race. In a powerful show of solidarity, he wore an Olympic Project for Human Rights badge, the same as Carlos and Smith, to support their protest. Though he didn't raise a fist, his quiet act of allyship cost him dearly back home, where he faced backlash and was left out of future Olympic selections despite qualifying. Then there was Florence Griffith-Joyner, who showed the world that women can be Black, fast and feminine as she set her two world records at Seoul 1988 in the 100m and 200m. These still stand as records almost forty years later.

This Black celebration of success through sport has continued through the years, up to now as I'm writing this, and will carry on into the future. At the Paris 2024 Olympics, Noah Lyles won one of the fastest 100m finals ever. The first ever men's Jamaican gold medal in the discus was achieved by Rojé Stona. The women's 100m final was a row of Black women and won by Julien Alfred from Saint Lucia. The GOAT (Greatest of All Time) herself, Simone Biles, won her team and all-around titles along with two other medals, including creating the iconic, first-ever all-Black podium in women's gymnastics. This is to say, sport is where you see us win. It's why I felt the sporting world was where I belonged and now, with running, why I'm so passionate about it as part of my identity.

Black Lives Matter

On 23 February 2020 at 1 p.m., Ahmaud Arbery went for a run in Glynn County, Georgia, and was chased by three white men in their trucks. Travis McMichael and his father, Gregory, accompanied by William Bryan, blocked him with their trucks as he tried to run away, firing shotgun blasts at close range to him. Travis overtook Ahmaud, stepped out of his truck and assaulted him and, while attempting to defend himself, Ahmaud was shot fatally.

He was just going for a run.

Not only was the act reminiscent of the lynching days gone past, but the behaviour by the police department and the district attorney following this was shocking. This act was caught on camera by William Bryan, but even with that evidence, the three men were not immediately arrested. It was only once the video was shared on social media two months later that a global outcry led to their arrests and eventual convictions. I was on social media when this news broke. As a runner, I felt sick to my stomach. Imagine if it was a friend, a brother, an uncle. As a Black person, we suffer trauma every time we see something like this brought to light. Imagine that you were just out running and your life was taken from you at twenty-five because of the colour of your skin.

The running community came out in force and ran 2.23 miles (representing the day his life was taken, 23 February) in Ahmaud's memory. Thousands of runners shared their runs on social media in support, using the hashtag #IRunWithMaud. It was a realization not just for Black people in the community but for everyone, that running isn't safe for all – especially for those who aren't white. For myself and many others, the murders of Black people are deeply traumatizing as we see ourselves and our families in these people. We see the world through a terrifying pair of binoculars.

During the coronavirus lockdown in 2020 and the world being on pause, the eyes of the people and the media were drawn to something 'never seen before'. By 'never seen before', what I mean is never *highlighted* before. Racism and racist acts have been non-stop throughout our society for centuries. Can these views ever change? I'd love to say yes, but we are a long way from that in many places around the world. In a moment of feeling powerless, running had the power to help bring about change – to bring people together for a moment, using the power of movement to celebrate and honour Ahmaud. I ran that 2.23 miles with tears in my eyes, and it helped me to remember the privilege I have to move freely.

The deaths of Ahmaud Arbery and George Floyd (who was killed by a police officer in 2020) reignited the Black Lives Matter movement on a scale akin to the Martin Luther King era. The race conversation and experiences that I had lived my whole life started to become mainstream topics. Finally, names of those who the Black community had lost to police brutality were being said and shared years after their deaths.

#SayTheirNames was the social hashtag that went viral during the Covid years of 2020–2021. The movement's goal was to prove not only that these deaths hadn't happened 'out of the blue' but also that Black Lives Matter. That the lives taken by officers should be known, and that those officers should be held accountable. Lives like Breonna Taylor, who was sleeping in her house when it was stormed by police on a raid and she was fatally shot. Like Philando Castile, who was pulled over in a traffic stop and was shot by an officer after stating he had a legal firearm in the car. Like Tamir Rice, a twelve-year-old boy playing with a toy gun who was shot on sight at a park.

The US is not the only country where young Black lives have been taken unjustly. On 4 August 2011 in the UK, Mark Duggan was stopped in his minicab and an officer shot him twice, claiming to have seen a gun. The gun in question was found seven metres from his body and no other officer spotted it. He was a Black man, and although the court ruled that Duggan was 'lawfully killed', there are large sections of the Black community who contest this ruling. His death revealed a type of racism predicated on the police perception of Black men as armed or criminal, leading to lethal force, force that arguably may not have been inflicted in the same way if he had been white.

On 5 September 2022, Chris Kaba was shot dead in Streatham, after being followed by police in a car. He was an unarmed Black man and was shot by officer Martyn Blake. His death shows the continuation of this racist pattern in the 2020s – despite decades of so-called 'reform'.

There's also one of the most discussed cases in the UK: Stephen Lawrence. He was murdered at a bus stop in 1993, by five men, only two of whom have been charged with murder, almost twenty years after his death. This failure in policing caused huge protests and outcry in the UK. Stephen was an unarmed Black man and was killed. The police's mishandling of the case exposed institutional racism within the Metropolitan Police, leading to the landmark Macpherson Report and widespread calls for reform. Stephen was both a victim of a racist murder by white civilians and also police failure to protect Black life. These are just some of the tens of thousands of innocent Black lives taken globally every year – their names should not be forgotten. Whether through police violence or police failure to act – racism in the system means Black lives aren't always given equal safety or justice.

Why have I told you all this? Why have we discussed race and these tumultuous times in history? Firstly, it's an important part of who I am and therefore how I've been shaped as an adult, and as a runner. Throughout 2020–2021, when the Black Lives Matter movement had become a huge part of the conversation, I used running in a way I hadn't before. To process my anxiety. To help figure out ways to vocalize my frustrations, to change my mood and, honestly, to use my platform on social media to promote a space for those who wanted to run but didn't have anyone who looked like them doing it. For me, running was habitual, a place I felt in control and at ease. When other areas of my life and the world were out of line, running was and is my safe space. I began to use my social platform as a way to help guide runners, many of whom had just taken up or rediscovered their love of running during the pandemic. Covid was both a curse and a blessing. To live through a pandemic was an out-of-body experience. The shift from going about day-to-day life to not leaving our homes, being terrified by the news and only being allowed outside for an hour of exercise a day feels very dystopian, looking back.

At first, when we went into lockdown, I was naively glad for a reset. I think, like many, I was clueless about the global severity of the situation at the time. I'd quit my full-time job as a footwear buyer two months earlier and had been running around London, beginning life as a self-employed group exercise instructor. I had permanent classes. I was teaching in a few gyms; I was working with clients one to one. I was juggling online content creation for brands, and I was speaking at events. I was everywhere all the time, excited for the year ahead. But you can see why the prospect of two weeks staying at home and working at a slower pace was a welcome break. Except it wasn't fine. I had minimal income, as some gyms couldn't afford to keep paying instructors, and it was a scary place to be. And then, of course, the lockdown lasted longer than any of us could have imagined. The mental health and wellbeing of society was at the forefront of media conversations. Once again, running came to the rescue. As many people didn't have equipment at home and the price of a pair of dumbbells had skyrocketed because everyone was sourcing them, many people donned their old runners and took themselves for runs.

For me, this time was a tough one to navigate mentally; I

was questioning my identity a lot, my race and my sexuality, and my mind was running ragged. So, I did what I knew how to do best: I ran, I lifted heavy things up and put them down, and I moved my body. The street where I lived during the lockdown had a dead end. It meant I could set up the extortionately priced dumbbells I'd managed to source and do strength sessions, as well as run without coming into contact with anyone. I used Instagram as a means to share my daily habits — not only to motivate but also to educate others on how to stay strong, as well as help keep them running throughout that time. This was everything from Q&As to home-made running plans which I created, called #RunThroughThis. The idea was to get people outside running and conquering even their first 5k or 10k or half marathon. #RunThroughThis created a community where every day people would share with me, and each other, the runs they'd conquered and their goals to run ten weeks later, using this plan as a vehicle to unite and bring people together through running in uncertain times. No matter who they were, their race, age, gender or size, it seemed that everyone was out running. The power of seeing people who looked like me running leans on that phrase I mentioned on page six and often come back to: *you can't be what you can't see.* Was this a time you considered running? Maybe it was the last time you actually ran, because you had no choice? Do you remember how it made you feel?

'Finding change' for me represents the way running builds identity. Because of my experiences of racism and 'otherness', I've been left unsure of my identity, but one thing that has really helped is running. It's helped me be proud of who I am in my skin, even if society still has an issue with it. Our world will hopefully continue to progress, and as it does, owning who you are instead of who society thinks you should be is so important. As some of my childhood experiences show, I was once scared to be who I was. I wanted to change parts of Emma to be more 'liked', more accepted and seen as more approachable to society. I wanted my hair to be smaller; I believed staying quiet in the face of racism was easier. Over the last few years, standing proud in my skin and with my big, natural hair (even though I still struggle to wear it not tied up) is something I've been forcing myself to do more. The more positive and sure you feel about yourself, the more it will drastically impact your motivation to take care of yourself and, ultimately, your desire to run.

FINDING AUTHENTICITY

As a child, running was where I found joy. As a teenager, I lost that joy and only ran when I needed to. The everyday ups and downs of teenage life — and my desire to be the best and so the turn to discus — put running, and that joy, on pause. After my dad died, running helped me process, work through my grief and begin to heal the wound of loss. Doing so slowly brought me back to that sense of joy. During lockdown, I needed that joy more than ever, to help keep the fear of what was happening in the world at bay. But on those runs in 2020 and 2021, I was also questioning another facet of who I was.

I'd taken a journey to find my authentic self and not just be 'her' internally but be proud to stand as 'her' in the big, wide world. I'd confronted my racial identity, and I'd worked through the experiences from my childhood. Why not dive head first into truly understanding my sexuality too? Questioning who I was attracted to was not something I paid too much attention to as a teenager or even into my early twenties. As with any teenager, I did have crushes growing up. Coupled with puberty plus trying to 'fit in' among my peers, my sexuality was never something I paid attention to. The rainbow flag that I should have been aware of was that the crushes I did have growing up were definitely for all genders. I remember hearing adults saying that during puberty, liking or being attracted to the same sex was a 'phase' and something you grew out of. Being bisexual was not validated or really understood. Even in queer, diverse Brighton, it was something that people saw as a midpoint in fully acknowledging that you were gay, not an endpoint. Back then, there was either gay or straight.

My first boyfriend was one of my best friends. He was a kind and wacky soul and we bonded over musicals and comedy skits. We even tried to start our own band at break times in the music room. 'Wonderwall' by Oasis was our go-to song to practise. He was always a little different from the other kids, getting in to school early so he could straighten his hair in the classroom. On many occasions, I questioned him on his sexuality, as any attempt at kissing between us felt forced and unnatural. We ended our relationship very quickly because he did realize he was gay. I'll never forget the words he texted me: *I used you as a guinea pig just to see ...*

Looking back now, I see how awful it must have been for him to try to come to terms with his sexuality. I remember watching him get bullied for years, being called all kinds of slurs. Even in a place seen as accepting, homophobia was still present. After we ended things, I was still his close friend. The feeling of hurt from our break up sat heavy within me, but I understood he was just figuring himself out. I was proud of him back then for being himself and standing proud in a school where children were mean and didn't like 'different'.

When I was going through my own questioning, I understood what he went through and now especially, my empathy for him has grown. There were huge shifts in my own personal understanding of myself during the lockdowns. I had begun to understand and process more of my racial identity, which felt empowering, but something still felt like it was missing. How could I look at just one part of my identity without addressing the other facets of who I am? As a newly self-employed person, my lockdown life consisted of waking up to run or train and then eating, working on my online business, then watching Netflix or TikTok, going to bed and repeating daily. I went from working all over London, clocking 20,000-plus steps a day, interacting with class members and commuting, to the silence of me, myself and my thoughts. The juxtaposition was huge, and with that came the time to think, to understand and look introspectively. With the increased time being spent behind a screen as the only way to connect to other people, I ended up jumping on the TikTok bandwagon, initially by making a fool of myself with the latest trends, performing some questionable dance moves and dramatic prose. As silly as it may sound, using this app is where my first true stage of examining my sexuality appeared.

For those who haven't used TikTok, the 'For You' page (also known in other apps as your homepage) uses an algorithm based on what you engage with most, as well as what is popular, to share videos on your homepage known as your feed. The algorithm kept sharing videos or images of lesbian and bisexual women on my feed. I engaged with them, and I did find many of them attractive. I remember noticing this, my brain going: *not me thinking she's good looking?* The algorithm would then take me to a video of a man I found attractive.

Confused.com.

All my dates, relationships and 'situationships' until this moment had exclusively been with men. I'd been happy in them, and I did truly feel emotionally invested in them – even in the ones where my heart got stamped on, too. There is no denying that over the years I'd been attracted to women on occasion, but I'd convinced myself it was never anything substantial. I definitely didn't think I was gay, and I didn't consider bisexuality as a reality.

In my new routine, my morning run helped me speak these thoughts into existence, a way to attempt to process this new-found information for myself. As my feet thudded against the ground, the internal dialogue would go a little like this:

What does this mean? Am I gay? I don't think I am because I still find men attractive, but also women, and I'm not sure how this is possible. Maybe I like women a little and men a lot – or maybe I don't like women at all; I just appreciate the way a woman looks and can admire her beauty. But also, I know that I'd happily kiss a woman I find attractive. Eek, did I just think that? But also, men can be beautiful, and in my past relationship, I did love him, I know that, and the chemistry was definitely there. But now, I'm looking at women in that same way . . . but then we wouldn't be able to have biological kids. It's complicated. And I want that for me but also, I like being

protected by a man and the idea of having that fairytale
family with him. I want to be looked after. I love that about
men who really care for a woman but also, I'm sure I like
women and I'm very sure a woman can do that for me
too, right? Oh man! Who the f*$k am I?!

This was a conversation that went round and round in my head (with extra expletives in there on occasion, too). I'd have to pause mid-run to breathe, walk and give myself space to process. There was a run I took that led down a river called the Wandle. After the wide opening, I sat on a park bench and, with the sun beating down on my face, the sounds of the water rushing through, I let a few tears slide down my face. The relentless repetition of my thoughts was consuming, like a slot machine constantly resetting and spinning, resetting and spinning with the win never coming. I was having a constant internal fight with myself about my bisexuality. Was I claiming bisexuality to avoid being gay? Or was there even a small part of me that believed it was a phase and I was still straight? When I wasn't running, these thoughts were so overwhelming. I didn't know where to start unpacking them. Longer runs allowed my mind to wander. Running for an hour allowed my heart rate and body to settle. The longer and the more I ran, the more at ease I felt with realizing I was attracted to both men and women.

It was day 823 of the first lockdown in the UK (okay, so it wasn't that long but it certainly felt like it). At the time, I lived in Colliers Wood in the south of London and had just returned from an invigorating morning run through the beautiful summer we were experiencing in 2020. Uninterrupted sunshine made the repetitive days manageable and the isolation just a touch easier. After showering, I collapsed on my bed, exhaling as if a lock on my chest had been opened and released the tension. On that run right there, I'd finally accepted it for myself:

I'm bisexual. It's not just a phase, I'm not confused – this is who I am.

When speaking to friends in my early twenties and conversations about being queer came up, I always remember piping up and saying, 'I believe everyone is on a sliding spectrum of sexuality. I don't believe anyone is truly 100 per cent straight or 100 per cent gay.' I look back now and chuckle to myself. No Emma, you were just a baby bi girl who even then was trying to work herself out! Now, my dialogue is more like this:

I'm bisexual. I'm attracted to people. I'm allowed to feel the confusion, but I now know this is my reality, and I get to shape how my romantic relationships look for the future. I'm proud of who I am, and anyone who doesn't stand by me in who I am and my relationships doesn't deserve to be in my circle.

When I was confident in my decision – that this identity was now my reality – I knew that telling someone would help me. Telling those I was closest to would allow me to bring my thoughts to reality. Through lockdown, I lived with my friend

Ella. We've known each other for twenty-plus years, from school. Growing up, in our early teens, we were more acquaintances than close friends, but during and after university we grew closer. To bring the reality of my bisexuality to life, I plucked up the courage to tell her (a solid half a bottle of wine deep to help steady the nerves). As soon as I said the words 'I think I like girls too', I burst into tears. I remember her saying, 'Is that it?' It was like air being released from a balloon. Our heads have a funny way of making a mountain out of a molehill, and gosh, did my brain do that! Ella said, 'It doesn't matter who you want to be with; as your friend, I just want you to be happy.' It made me sob even more. *It was okay to be me*. This new version of me that I had taken twenty-seven years on this earth to find. She was welcomed.

Speaking my sexuality into existence was a hard step but telling my close friends, my sister and mum, and hearing their total acceptance, was empowering. I'm so fortunate with how accepting my mum and sister were. I was afraid to tell them, but I knew they'd understand, and they did.

What I didn't predict was how hard I found it to accept myself – really accept myself. There is a difference between acknowledging something to be true and *actually* accepting and loving yourself for it; for the person you really are. Saying you're fine can be an easy answer to appease others, but *really* accepting yourself? That can be a path full of uneven surfaces and wild detours.

Internalized homophobia was a term I'd never heard of before I started speaking about it in therapy. It's what happens when a queer person directs society's negative attitudes around being gay or bisexual towards themselves and, in its extreme forms, can lead to the rejection of one's sexual orientation.[1] It's the idea that, throughout our lives, we are taught that a heterosexual romantic relationship is the only accepted way in society. That the only way to find happiness like in the movies is boy meets girl, they fall in love, get married, have kids and live happily ever after. Hearing and seeing negative depictions of the LGBTQ+ community can lead us to internalize those messages, no matter how much we want to shield ourselves. Never during the nineties, early 2000s, or rarely even now, do we see blockbuster films on queer couples existing or raising children. If you did back then, they weren't marketed boldly or, if they were, it became a breeding ground for homophobes to come out and attack. *Brokeback Mountain* is the only notable film I remember being in the spotlight, and I remember the absolute ruckus that it caused. Now, however, if you search for queer couples on social media, they are present, and more A-list celebrities are coming out and standing proud in who they are, and this will hopefully become more prevalent.

There is a darker, scarier side to the social media world, which is hard to not address. The comments section of many posts on news outlets or the wider social sphere of Twitter (X) or Instagram, when discussing LGBTQ+ issues or rights, is often not a positive place for a queer person to read. Keyboard warriors are vicious and will happily make queer and trans people feel irrelevant and unworthy by leaving defamatory and derogatory comments. I've worked with brands, promoting Pride Month and sharing what it means to me to be out and queer. I was disheartened to read the posts they shared through the month being slated and having hundreds of homophobic voices on them. As of 2024, sixty-four countries around the world continue to criminalize homosexuality, enforcing laws that target and marginalize individuals simply for who they are and who they love.[2] Among these, twelve countries have gone as far as to impose the death penalty as a possible punishment for same-sex relationships. Tragically, one of these countries is Nigeria, where my dad was from. Knowing this painful reality will always cut deep because it symbolizes not just a barrier to authenticity but a denial of my very existence. The thought that I can't freely express my true self in a country tied so closely to my heritage fills me with sadness and frustration. It's a stark reminder of how far we still have to go in the fight for equality and acceptance.

The reality of being queer has real and personal consequences that impact daily decisions in ways many others may not even have to consider. For instance, something as simple and joyous as planning a holiday becomes fraught with fear and uncertainty. Imagine researching potential travel destinations and having to ask yourself not about the sights, the food or the culture, but whether the country will accept your existence or force you to hide who you are. Imagine having to decide whether you and your partner can hold hands in public or must pretend to be 'just friends' or 'cousins' for your safety. This isn't about discomfort; it's about survival. It's about having to make calculated decisions to avoid becoming a target of violence or persecution, all because of something as fundamental as love.

The pain of this discrimination is twofold. On one hand, there is the personal impact of being unable to live authentically and love openly in certain spaces. On the other hand, there's the emotional toll of knowing that such laws and attitudes persist, reinforced by ignorance, hatred or deeply ingrained prejudice. For me, the fact that Nigeria, a place tied so deeply to my identity and my family, upholds such laws feels especially heartbreaking. It creates a divide between my heritage and my truth, forcing me to reconcile my love for my roots with the knowledge that I wouldn't be safe, welcome or free there as my true self. What's perhaps even more painful is the invisibility of this struggle to those who don't have to face it. For those of us within the LGBTQ+ community, these realities aren't hypothetical. They shape our lives, relationships and decisions every day. They remind us how privileged others are to move through the world without fear of persecution for their identity. But they also remind us of the importance of continuing to advocate for change. The fight for equality is far from over, and until every person, no matter where they live, can love and live freely, there will always be work to do. This isn't just a political issue; it's a human one. It's about dignity, safety and the right to exist without fear. Not making a change reinforces the validation of internalized homophobia, which I know I'll continue to work on now. Back in 2020, I had to do this swiftly because I met Clare.

Clare came into my life before the second lockdown of 2020 in the UK. I won't turn this into a romance novel, but I'll tell you about the beginning of our relationship. We worked for the same gym, and our company, like many, began offering online workouts. A handful of instructors would write the workouts for the team and others would create a playlist, and we'd collectively do them together via Zoom. Clare wrote the majority of the workouts and led many of the sessions. I was a newish instructor to the team, so she messaged me one day and asked if I wanted to write the next workout. I did. Many online workouts later, we met in real life when the gyms reopened. There was a connection between us, a spark. Like how every time she smiled, I wanted to hear the words her brain was saying. Like how her face was saying so much with an expression that I wanted to know more, but was afraid to ask. I knew it was more than friendship, and I felt the constant need to speak to her and be around her all the time. When I wasn't with her, I wondered what she was doing and when I'd see her next.

Was this me, bisexual Emma, attracted to a real-life girl? Three days before the lockdown in December 2020, we had our first date. We moved in with each other for Christmas as we couldn't travel home to family: the classic lesbian stereotype of U-Hauling on the second date. Clare was similar to me. We both had never been in a relationship with a woman and had only dated men all our lives. She identifies as pansexual and loves people, whoever they are, for simply who they are – attracted to a soul rather than a body. Some of you may have started your relationships in lockdown, and there was a beauty to that. We were thrust into each other's lives, and as women who were strong-minded, emotional communicators, we navigated so much in our early relationship. The closeness and love that came so quickly in those first few months made everything overwhelming. I wanted to be around her all the time, hugging her, cooking food with her, training with her, just being with her.

Running was and still is so wonderfully intertwined within our relationship. We lived about 11 miles away from each other, so occasionally we would run to each other's houses during lockdown. I have a memory of her running to me during heavy snowfall. To truly appreciate this, you need to understand one thing about Clare. She's what I lovingly call 'geographically challenged'. You may have some people like this in your life, ones who have walked down the same street multiple times yet still manage to get lost when left to their own devices. That's Clare. Instead of an 11-mile run, it became an epic 13.5-mile detour to my flat. I opened the door to a drowned, wind-blown, drenched human being with snow clinging to her jacket like icing sugar dusted on a cake and hair plastered against her face. Her bottom lip jutted out in a mix of exhaustion and triumph, and with a little shudder running through her voice, she managed to say, 'I made it.' I burst out laughing. There she was, my determined, albeit directionally challenged, Clare who had just braved a snowstorm to come and spend time with me. I flung the door open, ushered her in and squeezed some warmth into her. This was one of the moments I realized I was falling for her. This didn't just happen once, either.

I was falling in love, and I was falling hard. Was I scared? Oh, absolutely terrified. My mind thought of things I could do to make her day or experience better all the time. It was all-consuming in the best ways possible. By the time I finally told Clare I loved her, I wanted to make it special and use my words. I wrote her a letter. In it, I tried to put the depths of my feelings into words. This letter was one of the simplest and most freeing things I've written. I was finally sure of my emotions and feelings and completely unafraid to share that fact. I told her that something in the universe had conspired to bring us together, that it felt like this was always part of the plan, even if neither of us could have foreseen it growing up. I poured my heart into that letter and told her the truth that had been bubbling up inside me for weeks: I loved her. I loved a woman. I was beaming with the warm, fuzzy feeling you hear about in the movies, and it was all because of her. Clare had not only captured my heart but had also opened a door to a kind of love I never knew was possible: a love full of humour, compassion, resilience and the kind of warmth that lingers long after the snow melts.

Lockdown did not last forever, and life (thank goodness) began to return to normal. I struggled so much with our transition into everyday life out of lockdown – we both did. We now had to exist in the big, wide world, together. A judgemental world. When I shared my post on social media coming out, I felt a weight lift. My social media accounts were something I'd always been completely myself and honest on. Coming out there was the first step to stepping back into the big, wide world with my new identity. Here's the text from the post I shared in 2021:

When you find your person, it doesn't matter who they are.

She makes me laugh and grin ear to ear. Through this lockdown, she's seen every side of me and yet is still by my side. She might be a faster runner than me on occasion, but I'm stronger haha! She's helped me find my true self and she's helped me not be scared to accept who I truly am.

She's special.

I won't lie to you. It's been hard for me to want to share this... I don't know why. Yes, it's my personal life, but I strive to be my honest self on this platform... so here I am! It's the happiest I've ever been yet... I had the fear. Fear of judgement? Fear of being my authentic truest self I possibly can be? Vulnerability? Being hyper aware of being mixed race and bi and now navigating the world? Maybe accepting again that I don't have it all figured out as I thought I did? The truth – most definitely all of the above.

But hey, here I am, my authentic self: a strong, happy woman supported and in love with another strong fierce woman. Come at us world I dare you.

Be you, always. Don't shrink who you are because of fear of judgement; because hey, why would you want to be anyone else!

That last line of judgement is ironic because the fear of judgement I had about coming out was consuming me. My biggest struggle, one both of us still have conversations about, was being affectionate in public. In previous heterosexual relationships, I didn't mind being outwardly affectionate, but I found it hard with Clare. It felt like I was arguing with my own shadow, full of frustration towards myself. Maybe I was embarrassed?

Maybe I was worried about how people around me would react? Deep down, some part of me also didn't want to potentially offend those around me. Even writing that feels strange. It's something that even now, I work through daily, weekly, to feel confident in: being in a lesbian relationship and being affectionate. In some situations in the past, I'd even question wanting to hold Clare's hand. I'd question giving her a peck on the cheek, let alone the lips, in a public setting. I had true fear of being 'out' in the world.

Along with all the joy and discovery that came with falling in love with Clare, one of the struggles I had to face was coming to terms with my sexuality and, in doing so, mourning the 'fairytale ending' I had always envisioned for myself. By that, I mean the idea of the picture-perfect romance, something we're constantly fed by the media and pop culture, especially growing up in the late nineties and early 2000s. Back then, all the romantic ideals and happy endings revolved around a man and a woman. The movies I watched, the stories I grew up with, all painted this very particular version of what love should look like, and that vision was deeply ingrained in me. Films like *Sleepless in Seattle*, *Notting Hill* and *10 Things I Hate About You* were the epitome of romance, filled with grand gestures and neatly tied bows at the end. Especially Disney, which shaped so much of my childhood, had iconic couples like Aladdin and Jasmine, Tarzan and Jane, and, of course, Belle and her Beast. These stories were everywhere, and they quietly reinforced what I thought my life and my love story would look like: a prince, a happily-ever-after and everything falling perfectly into place.

Falling in love with Clare meant unlearning societal norms and detaching myself from those ideals. It wasn't just about embracing my sexuality, it was about accepting that my love story wouldn't look like the ones I grew up dreaming about. And, at first, that was hard. It was hard to let go of this image I'd built in my mind since I was a little girl. It felt, in some ways, like grieving the version of my life I thought I'd have. Clare and I often talk about how our relationship doesn't fit into traditional moulds, and that's part of what makes it so special. This didn't come naturally to us straight away, and even we had to unlearn our expectations of one another. Instead, we've carved out our own way of existing together. We've created a space where we decide what works for us, where there's freedom to grow and love on our own terms. There's no blueprint for who should propose first (I did), or what our future 'should' look like. There's only what we want it to be, and that's something we're still figuring out together.

Our proposal story was planned, but not entirely. In December 2024, we were down in Brighton for the weekend visiting my mum ahead of Christmas. Clare woke up that first morning and said, 'Emma, I want us to get rings today.' Now, this wasn't out of the blue. Having been together nearly four years, we had spoken about the fact we wanted to get engaged and married – it was just a matter of when. But still, her bold statement gave me a little jolt – *Ah, we're really doing this*. My eyes widened and an uncontrollable grin sprang across my face. 'Let's do it.' I beamed. It had been Clare's idea for my mum to be involved and present when we chose our rings, which was a lovely touch. Plus, doing it in Brighton just felt right. In Brighton, queer couples are almost the norm, so walking into a jeweller's hand in hand and saying we wanted rings was met with 'Oh fantastic – do you both know what you'd like? Let us show you all our options', rather than the fear of being judged elsewhere. Once selected and acquired, the last conversation we had on the topic of who was to propose was more about whoever goes first. I began my plans to be the one to propose in January of 2025. It began with asking a good photographer friend of ours to hide, as I had planned to propose in front of London's Tower Bridge. I gathered some of our closest friends to be at a brunch spot I had organized post-proposal, plus created a sneaky undercover story with her best friend to get her to the location. On 8 March, on International Women's Day no less, I proposed to Clare Rafferty and asked if she'd be my wife. To my surprise, she had *my* ring in her bag and so proposed to me at the exact same time. I can honestly say it was, and is (until we get married), the happiest day of my life!

Unlearning those societal expectations and dismantling those pre-existing ideals hasn't been easy. It's a process, one that requires constant reflection and questioning of what we've been taught to believe about love and relationships. But as challenging as it's been, it's also been liberating. Letting go of those rigid ideas has made room for something far more authentic and beautiful: a relationship that's truly ours. It's not about fitting in to anyone else's version of a fairytale; it's about creating our own. And even if it doesn't look like the love stories we grew up with, it's perfect in its own way. Being Black and queer is a space that, even to this day, I'm continually learning to lean in to. It's a new space I'm trying to find my footing in. To feel represented and find others that I see myself in, I try to use social media to follow athletes, actors and actresses, as well as friends in my running community, who I can seek inspiration and joy from. I recently saw the film *Wicked* and I cried, not just as I'm a theatre lover but also for another reason. Cynthia Erivo depicting Elphaba made me feel so seen. Her portrayal as a queer Black woman, of being 'other' and yet leaning in to herself, was monumental for not only film but queer Black people. *You can't be what you can't see.*

Beneath the noise of societal expectations, buried under my own fears, insecurities and the grief of peeling back the layers of my identity, I found something rare – a moment of quiet. Running gave me that. It wasn't just movement – it was a way to listen. With each step, I started to untangle the mess in my head, to hear my own voice more clearly. I remember the snowstorm; how Clare ran to me through it, intentionally, so we could see each other. That act, so simple yet bold, felt like a proclamation of love. It reminded me that running isn't just for fitness or escape, it's a form of expression. It's choosing to show up, in all your layers, all your questions. And we should all be free to express ourselves that way without apology. No matter what some people may say, sexuality is not a choice. You don't wake up one day and decide 'I want to be queer'. Think about going out for a run. You head out the door, and there's a natural running stride you have. There's a natural rhythm your body falls into unconsciously. A way your right foot will always rotate out, or a way your heart rate will always increase from your rested state when you run. These are things you have no conscious control over. Just like sexuality.

Some people may embrace you. Some people may not understand. They may even reject you and who you are becoming because it makes them feel uncomfortable — something I recently experienced with a family member when I shared our engagement. What did I turn to in that moment, when I felt judged and unheard? Running. In understanding my sexuality, running as a tool never spoke back. It wasn't like a person who could give an opinion (wanted or unwanted). Running gave me and my mind space. When figuring out your identity — and in this case, sexuality — sometimes you just need space. I needed the silence, the simplicity of hearing my feet brush along the road, the constant sound of my breath as I worked through all the questions racing through my head.

Running didn't give me an answer or an opinion. It was just there for me to use when I needed it. It helped by giving me a reminder: you will always find true peace with accepting who you are first and how that presents itself in your own reality. Authenticity may not always be easy, but finding it is the foundation for true contentment.

FINDING COMMUNITY

Traditionally, running has been seen as an individual sport, and for many, this can be the case. Some of you who already run may prefer running alone and the simple solitude it brings. But in some of the biggest cities, that solitude is easily found. London gives the illusion that everyone is hustling all the time, that people have many friends that they *kiki* with on the weekends, that we're all thriving, living in this cosmopolitan metropolis. For many, that may be the case. A large number of people, however, including myself, do feel and have felt lonely. There is a strange solitude in many aspects of this city; from the silence on packed tubes, to the bustle of commuters power-walking through the streets to their office blocks, eyes on the pavement, head down and with very minimal interaction with the world around us.

As friends moved on in their respective lives and relationships, I felt loneliness deep to my core on many occasions, notably in my early twenties when living in Mitcham. Being lonely is a vulnerable thing to acknowledge, a terrifying thing to admit to others and yourself, especially when you live in a big city, surrounded by people all of the time. I worked as a coach and was seeing people often but these were surface-level acquaintances, not the deep connections I needed. And this is normal. As humans we are social creatures, craving purposeful interactions. The answer? Try to foster communities. This is one of the reasons running has skyrocketed in popularity. The boom of running and run clubs has fed that growing sense of belonging so many are in need of. Running has been a catalyst for connection for many.

Like any other big city, London is expensive, and with that comes the stress of worrying about having enough money to live on. As a thirty-something-year-old, it feels like many people are working on their craft, operating long, unsociable hours just to pay their rent and bills. To have a social life on top of that is an added expense and also hard to prioritize when you are exhausted, which then leads to more loneliness. Do you go to the pub and spend £10 on a glass of wine? No, thank you. Or, with the rise of people not drinking alcohol, what spaces are there that don't involve drinking? We are also all now accustomed to interacting via screens, which doesn't have the same quality as seeing and speaking to a real-life human. I'd wake up and check my phone, open socials, scroll, open WhatsApp looking for someone to message, then doomscroll again on TikTok, and soon I'd have lost three hours of my life and be thinking: *what do I do now?* This is all a breeding ground for feeling alone, even in the big city.

This loneliness epidemic isn't just limited to London. Recent studies, including research from the Campaign to End Loneliness, have confirmed that it's a public health crisis that adds huge pressure to the mental health sector. [1] Running initially gave me a sense of freedom from the isolation I'd developed from working all the hours and not wanting to be social. As clichéd as it sounds, it started with a simple step to get outside. Since that day in September when I'd found myself again through running, I had continued to run weekly, mostly alone and for that mental headspace. I didn't really identify myself as a runner until I found Nike Run Club (NRC). Ironically, it was only when I stopped working at Nike that I actually had time to join my first-ever run club.

In 2015, I went along for the first time. I didn't expect to be nervous, but as I approached the gathering group outside the Covent Garden store, I felt a twist in my stomach. The nerves were around the idea of meeting new runners. What if I wasn't fast enough? What if I got left behind on the run? My mind urged me to turn around and walk away but my legs kept going. As I went to pull the door handle to the store, a person arrived right next to me, clearly clocking me in my running kit, and smiled, opened the door and said through beaming teeth, 'You look ready to run!' Nike's idea was simple: bring like-minded people together, run while giving varied pace options and have fun. In the initial years while NRC was small, they had an incentive which engaged my inner competitor. If you ran at ten different Nike Running events, you would receive a t-shirt with the word 'RUNNER' written across it. I knew this was going to be mine. Week in, week out, I ran with them at Covent Garden. I took track sessions in East London and from NTL (NikeTown London). I received my t-shirt ten runs later and was given it by the then head coach, Becs Gentry. The shirt represented more than just ten attendances for me. It represented an identity which I'd harnessed but also a community I felt fully and unequivocally welcomed into. People wanted to know my name, my background, how I found out about NRC, and as I left, the most inclusive phrase in that moment was said: 'See you next week!' I couldn't stop grinning as I left. I knew I was part of something – it was a community I had been long craving.

I ran religiously with NRC for two years and made many like-minded friends, as we'd all been brought to running through similar experiences – either to overcome depression, loss, loneliness or find our purpose. We all had busy working lives outside in the world but when it came to nights running, we were all able to have fun, switch off and just *be*. The joy and fun I'd felt as a kid was coming back as a grown adult, the sensation of running felt like sun on my face. I was surrounded by other big kids on every run. Over the years, we did elevated events with GB track stars like Dina Asher-Smith, we turned car parks into off-road race tracks and shut down London streets to celebrate the 2016 Nike Olympians home. They were some of the best experiences I've had through running in my life. So much so, that I had the honour to be asked in 2017 if I wanted to be a Nike Pacer.

A pacer's role was to guide and lead runners who showed up to run club. Whether on the athletics track, local parks or around the streets of London. I didn't think twice. The thought that I could be a leader and guide for other runners, to find their passion, was something very close to my heart. It was my first taste of coaching, and I adored it. For the first time in a long while, I was in a group of people and communicating and not feeling lonely. I felt heard by their intention to ask about who I was, cared for as they waited for me when I stopped mid-run to tie a shoelace, and seen when in our group photo I wasn't the only person of colour; for once I wasn't the minority. I know I come alive when in a group setting, dating back to my netball-loving days. It makes even more sense as to why I now teach group exercise classes. I thrive on supporting others in a group setting. Do you feel it too?

It's not just a coincidence. Science backs up the importance of community and how it can help you to feel like you belong. Our very early ancestors lived and functioned in group settings. Anthropologists explain how social bonds were how the human race survived in the early years of our life.[2] The support of family and building friendships and power dynamics helped us to thrive. The same goes for today. So many areas in which we achieve success are built upon having a team around you that have the same interests, goals and beliefs. Running groups and communities are no different. A 2022 study by Franken, Bekhuis and Tolsma, published in *Frontiers in Sports and Active Living*, found that when running in a group, not only are we more likely to stick to our training habits but also we are more likely to hit our training goals.[3] Meaning, being surrounded by other people helps us to achieve. Furthermore, in a study in 2022 in the Journal of Behavioural Medicine, Carolyn Plateau and her colleagues found that beginners who joined running communities had highly positive mental benefits from running in a group setting.[4] From self-efficacy (confidence) improvements to bettering chances of participation and reducing social anxiety, running and community go hand in hand. These papers all confirm the idea that working/running in a group can bring increased positive mental health benefits compared with running alone. NRC was a powerful movement.

From the NRC days to continuing to share my running on social media, an audience found me and I them. In the early days of social media, it felt like it was all about building each other up. I began diligently sharing my training, my challenges, and connecting with other motivated individuals on social media. I was able to find a community of people who valued fitness, running, and were also training for the same races globally. It didn't have to be a person in the same local run club as me in London, it could be anyone in the world. It felt incredible to socially connect with people who didn't even speak the same language as I did. But to comment a word of support or send them congratulations on their running journey felt like we were all connected through our shared passion. Running was about to take me on an international, communal adventure.

I was invited by the running brand Saucony to be involved in a commercial they were creating out in Denver, Colorado called *Why We Run*. The scale of this commercial was huge. I couldn't believe that little old me was getting to do something so vast. The concept of the advert was about bringing runners from around the world together to meet in the early hours of the morning and take on a challenging run in the mountains. I met a group of people and all I knew about them was that they loved running and it had changed their lives, just like it had for me. Lecia was from Canada, Manu from South America, Justine from France, Promoe from Sweden and Rich was from the UK too. We filmed across three days throughout Golden in Colorado, from sunrise all the way through sunset. There were many epic shots of us running through the tundra and winding roads to the mountains.

One memory that I'll never forget was the final ascent at Loveland Pass. Loveland is the highest mountain pass in Colorado, standing at 3,655m above sea level. All of us sprinted up a rocky narrow way in the road to ascend to a breathtaking panoramic view of the mountains. They rolled in layers on the horizon, like a watercolour painting with the earth and sky blending seamlessly. Breathtaking both literally and metaphorically, as the air up there was pretty thin. We made it to the top and as part of the scene in the commercial had to look out at the view and congratulate each other. Nothing felt more natural than that moment. That we were all from all different walks of life but in that moment, we were there because we simply enjoyed and believed in the power of running.

As the sun set that evening, we all stayed to watch and soak up the experience. I remember taking a huge inhale to breathe in this moment and looking out in front of me to try and screenshot the view in my mind. I thought of all the places running had taken me, all the doubts I'd started my first run with, the emotions I'd carried when I ran to Dad's red door, never imagining it'd take me to this mountain top. As I exhaled, I turned to the others and could see the same feeling on many of their faces. We discussed how magical this moment was for us all. That every single one of our decisions had led us to now, this moment. I had always known running had the power to connect me to others, but this trip was a stark reminder of that.

On my return to the UK, another running community was born, one I was proud to have a direct impact with: Track Life LDN (TLL). Track Life began back in 2018 as the Nike Run Club events died down due to a restructure on Nike's behalf, and Rory Knight and Omar Mansour came together to bring track back to life in South London. They had both been coaches of the NRC track sessions I'd co-led with them as a pacer. They invited me to join the two of them in the coaching team, which I was chuffed by. The premise of TLL was to break down barriers of fear to those getting on the track for the first time and to show runners that track is for everyone. A track is a circular 400m course, made of a specific material, where historically athletics meets take place, or you may remember elevated sports day trips to a track as a child. A track is actually bouncier than the regular road, but can definitely be a more intimidating space.

We had over one hundred runners show up to the first event we hosted, with runners who ran four-minute miles or twelve-minute miles taking part in the session. The group that I coached after our warm-up drills was 'sexy pace'. Have you ever feared showing up to a running event or club, worried you might be too slow? Intimidated by other runners speeding on past and barging you out the way? These are stories I've heard from many 'back of the pack' runners. As much as we want to glamorize running, this can happen to many, so within

Track Life LDN we created 'sexy pace'. 'Sexy pace', which was also used in NRC, is a party pace for people who show up for enjoyment, not necessarily to be the fastest track-side but instead to better themselves. We refused to call our runners 'slow' because speed is relative. Every pace deserves a place.

In our first few years, we met an array of runners. For some of our teams, there were children as young as nine coming to run track during the summer holidays. There was also an incredible gentleman named Jonathon who would come and join us in the autumn months. Jonathon was seventy years old and lived alone. He would come to track when he could make it and run alongside the twenty- to thirty-year-olds and show them how it was done. He was such a wonderful man, and I'll never forget him saying how welcomed he felt by the group: 'We all just love to run so why would the group intimidate me, we are all just doing what we love together.' That's the power of running. Track Life LDN has continued to grow over the last six years, continuing to hold weekly track sessions and large summer events with a focus on educating and bettering the community at the forefront. My life was enriched by becoming a coach with TLL and it was another step in reducing my loneliness and feeling less lost. Track Life connects people through the simple idea of removing a key barrier to entry: fear. It lets people know that track can be for everyone and with that brings this brilliant sense of community and of overcoming the things that scare us. It's a place where I met one of my closest friends and one where I know so many friendships continue to be forged.

Social media can also offer this running community. Using

social media channels such as Instagram, YouTube, Strava and TikTok, you can find information on races you are looking to do and also connect with other runners taking on the same run. For every race I have ever entered, I've searched the hashtag of the race itself and celebrated what others posted. This may be other runners' wins, giving them kudos on their furthest run ever, or empathizing when I see they've struggled. And we all do! It's the power of community, both in person and online, that continues to make running special. These relationships are vital to our contentment as humans. Time and life challenges can make it hard to always train with others or be in a group setting. Social media, when used for good, can really be a lifeline to people who seek that connection not only to themselves but also to others through their runs.

Two great examples of this are, at a grass-roots level, parkrun, and in the marathon running space, the World Marathon Majors. Parkrun takes place across the world on a Saturday morning and is the definition of community. It was founded back in 2004 by Paul Sinton-Hewitt and a small group of runners coming together to run around Bushy Park in Teddington on an autumnal October morning. The concept is simple: run a free 5k at any pace around the park every weekend. For their first run, they had only five volunteers and a stopwatch. For two years, they stayed at Bushy Park before expanding and gosh, did they do that. As of 2025, parkrun now takes place at over 2,300 events worldwide. A space that encourages everyone to show up and devote time to themselves through the power of running. Every single runner or walker in parkrun is welcomed. No one is left behind so no matter how 'slow' you think you are, people will be there for you. The community is well known for 'parkrun on tour' where they tour the country and the world taking on different runs.

One of the things that brought me joy is that they celebrated the fact that the average 5k finish time dropped from 22:17 in 2005 to 32:30 in 2020. This shows the inclusion of every kind of runner's ability and the truly empowering initiative parkrun has become. To this day, there is no time cap on the weekly event, and there are tail-walker volunteers who walk with those at the back of the pack as a community. Junior parkrun now also exists: a 2k run for those aged four to fourteen. This community truly has the power to change lives. To create habits and encouragement for the youth to move via the motion of running but also for everyone, young and old, to turn up for free, week in, week out. Have you taken part in a parkrun? It's something I always wanted to do, however, since the age of thirteen, I've always worked on a Saturday. As of 2024, I stopped doing so, and I recently took on my local parkrun, and what struck me most wasn't the distance or the pace – it was the *energy*. There was no pressure to perform. It didn't matter if you were chasing a PB (personal best) , running with your dog or walking the whole thing. Every step was met with encouragement, every volunteer cheered like you were winning. The sense of community was genuinely heartwarming – from 16-year-olds full of bounce to 70-year-olds striding with quiet determination. Parkrun really is for everyone, no matter where you're starting from. Parkrun is for you.

The World Marathon Majors is the name for the seven

(eighth and ninth pending at date of writing) most prestigious marathon races around the world. In completing all of them, you receive a medal commemorating the achievement, and for many, these races serve as a bucket-list achievement for their running prowess. I'm one of those hunting down these stars. The seven marathons are currently: London, Berlin, Tokyo, Chicago, New York, Boston and Sydney. Both Hong Kong and Cape Town are awaiting their confirmation. Out of the fifteen marathons I've completed, I currently have three (Berlin, Chicago and London) of the stars, and they are incredible races in their own right.

Running Chicago was memorable as it was Clare's first marathon (I told you I'd get her to run one). The city came out in their millions to be our energy boost on race day. The day before the Chicago marathon, we met an inspiring man at a 5k race. His name was Nico. Nico was sixty-six, and we met him in an initially frantic state. We were trying to find the start line, darting up and down a 300m stretch of road. He could see that we were lost and as he walked past, he yelled, 'This is the way to the start, come on, follow me.' He was short but athletic, his salt-and-peppered beard giving him a wise and distinguished look, and he radiated enthusiasm. He wore a purple Northwestern top and on his feet he wore a pair of very well-loved trainers. We both instantly felt safe with him.

During this 5km run, we came to learn that the next day's Chicago marathon was Nico's sixty-third 26.2 miles he'd raced. He had fallen in love with the sport as a young man and continued to run his entire life, telling us that the marathon had changed his life. He explained that some of the races he was most proud of were those where he helped others to the finish, where he paced friends or helped people out at the roadside mid-race. He was such a jovial character, and every time Clare talked, he would try to mimic her Ayrshire accent, which he did very successfully. As the 5k started, we thought we'd lose Nico and so we bid him farewell. As the race began and we headed down the expansive Columbus Drive, the buzz of the city traffic was transformed into cheering crowds. The tall metropolitan city put on a show as local bands adorned the street, creating a rhythmic, melodic hum that carried all of us through the city.

At three kilometres, we turned the corner only to be running past the iconic Opera House and there was Nico, his purple t-shirt shining like a beacon. He took the time and energy to tell us about the history of the Opera House, and once our tour guide was finished, he waved us on to the finish. This time we really did bid each other farewell and wished him all the best for Sunday's marathon. We didn't see him on marathon day but that interaction with him brought so much joy to both of us. Nico had lived his life simply. Running for the community, running to meet people like ourselves from all walks of life. Chicago was Nico's penultimate marathon, and he had decided his sixty-fourth would be his last-ever race, in Athens in November 2024. He said it was time to hang up the shoes. Secretly, we both hope he has changed his mind. The Chicago marathon was one of my favourite races of all time. There's something about the support of an American crowd in a sporting situation that feels like you have extra propulsion with every step. Not only their cheers, but their constant offering of food, music, hydration – even shots of tequila en route (no, I didn't take one) made the energy like momentum to keep you driving to the finish line. And what a privilege it was to run Clare's first marathon with her.

The London Marathon is my home marathon. Growing up, it was one of the first big races, aside from the Olympics, that I remember watching on the television. Seeing Paula Radcliffe sprint down the Mall to a new world record of 2:15:25 is emblazoned in my mind. It was incredible watching people lining the streets to cheer and wish other people the best. When I was eighteen, I entered the ballot for the London Marathon, not having a clue what I was putting myself up for. Luckily for me then, I didn't get a place. But almost every year since I was twenty-one, I have entered the ballot. As is the luck with ballots, to this day I've never gotten in through it. However, through my job as a Footwear Buyer in 2018, New Balance gave me the opportunity to take part, and I was ecstatic. It was also going to be my fourth marathon. For those who have never done the race, it's 26.2 miles through London, starting in Blackheath in South-East London and then meandering through the city, over the famous Tower Bridge, to the banking district of Canary Wharf and finishing past the Houses of Parliament and Big Ben, down towards the iconic Mall in front of Buckingham Palace.

It was race morning. I'd put in weeks of training to be able to get to the start line. Which, side note, is one of the most incredible things to be able to do. Everyone talks about the end product of racing. In reality, surviving the countless days training leading to an event and being able to start on the line healthy is a huge achievement. Shout-out to you if you've made it to any start line. The London Marathon has three start colours: red, blue and green. They all have different closest train stations and, for the first 3 miles, a different start to the iconic race. In 2018, I was red start. I had no idea what I was in for and headed to London Bridge to catch the train. I had controlled everything I could: my kit, my shoes, my post-race clothes, my fuel. Yet I was still nervous, bouncing my knees up and down in anticipation. The train station on marathon Sunday was wild. I was advised to get there early, and it was the best advice I could have received. Thousands of runners were attempting to board trains and all crammed in like sardines in a can. But the beauty in it all was the runners. I spoke to so many people, all of us chatting away, questioning the weather, wondering if we'd make it on the next train and mentally already making plans B, C and D just in case something went wrong. In a very British fashion, we all queued politely. I had to let three trains full of people go before I could sardine myself into a carriage.

When we arrived, the streets were already teeming with runners consuming bananas and replacing their shoes for the twentieth time. Families were walking with rucksacks full of supplies, adorned with homemade signs ready to cheer on strangers. I walked past countless dogs, one with a sign that said, 'emotional support dog for runners'. Iconic. Once I had arrived at the bag drop, I was greeted by countless runners who shared with me that they'd followed my journey to race day or that they'd been helped by the content I'd shared. It was a humbling moment, as I realized that my journey online that started as a training diary had resonated with people in real life and my words and advice had actually made a difference. That was the reason I'd begun sharing my story, to keep me accountable but most importantly, to try to help others with my knowledge. I hadn't even crossed the start line, and my heart was full.

There were big screens showing information of why people were running and who they were doing it for. Some running in memory of lost parents, others running to aid in the thousands of important charities helping to prevent cancer, Alzheimer's, and to support children's hospices, to name a few. Hearing these stories, my eyes filled with tears, but I held it together. I wasn't going to release those floodgates just yet. In the start pens, we were all a little nervous, as the temperatures were warm. We applied sun cream last minute, in true running fashion, sharing it around. Vaseline, a runner's best friend, was also being passed around the corral to lube up thighs and nipples. As soon as the gun went off, given the temperatures, I decided I didn't care about the time I got and this run was all about London, about soaking up all the moments of this race. I high-fived every hand I could. I took sweets from strangers. I got shot at by water guns from people's houses trying to cool us all down. I cheered on other runners around me and also walked to cool down and soak up the many moments.

One of the many things the London Marathon is known for, aside from its incredible support, is its running crews. The London running scene, as with many around the world, has boomed in recent years, and come race day every running community comes out with the mantra: 'if you don't run you cheer'. Since I began running, everyone told me about mile twenty-one, notoriously when energy levels can drop and you can meet the 'wall'. However, in London, that point is where the legendary Run Dem Crew sets up. Cheer Dem, as they are also known come marathon day, are a community of runners founded by Charlie Dark MBE, an OG for the running culture of London running communities. Running through this section was like having rocket jets put onto the back of you. When I saw their friendly faces, and confetti cannons went off, it was a real high. And the hype isn't just for the fast runners that come shooting through. The running crews stay out for every runner, right to the back of the pack, once again, showing care for everyone. Showing that every runner matters, no matter their pace, age, race or ability.

One part of the London Marathon that I remember from 2023, is Rainbow Road. Rainbow Road is around mile twenty-two of the race where, when you need it most, you are completely uplifted by the queer community. The road is a long rainbow with giant multi-coloured flags lining the barriers, with people from the LGBTQ+ choir out singing and dancing for the runners. It continued for a good 200m down the street. On the final turn, as the rainbow road ended, there was a huge stage where drag acts were singing and cheering us all on. To see a community that I was part of celebrate the other love in my life (running) was really emotional. Tears filled my eyes and I let out a 'YAS' and bounded past the drag queen, waving at her like a four-year-old at Disney World. I felt so proud to have battled to find myself and realized I could be whatever and whoever I want. I knew that running would accept me and celebrate me for just that.

London finishes as you run down the Mall. As you turn onto it, you run under a bridge which reads '385 yards to go'. Then, adorned with union jack flags, while crowds scream for you and your successes, the finish line awaits. Nothing can describe a finish-line feeling. Pride, joy, pain, relief, fatigue, adrenaline, excitement – all rolled into one. I cried when I crossed that line in 2018. I cry at most marathon finish lines.

Running is a powerful way to bring people together, no matter if you're running on a course or are on the sidelines. Nothing compares to race day. There are thousands of runners that are running with you but also a constant wall of noise from thousands of spectators who are simply there because they want you to win. Those spectators aren't always just in a race setting. They may be the online community; the ones lining your local parkrun or the volunteers who simply take part in events because of what running means to them. They're cheering because they want you to succeed.

Nowhere else in our day-to-day life does that exist. Imagine a stranger clapping you for making it through your work day. With the marathon, it's simply a given. Your marathon may be just getting the shoes on and making it out the door before work. Your cheer squad can be people in your family, or friends. Let them know about the journey you're on. You may not even ever be considering running as far as a marathon, but it's an experience I believe every person should have. The best of humanity shows up on a marathon day to cheer. It's a community like no other, and one I'm so unbelievably proud to be a part of and invite you to be part of too.

Running towards and for community was a reason I continued to run. Without that backbone of people around me who did what I loved to do, I don't know if I'd have developed my passion as much as I have today. If you're starting your journey and you're uninspired or struggling to find the consistency and motivation, find others to do it with. Running alone is a way to start. Running together is a way to continue.

FINDING HEALING

It was an ordinary morning – or so I thought. British summer, in all its unpredictable glory, had opted for a grey, wet start. Instead of sunshine warming my skin, rain sliced through the air and dull clouds hung heavy in the sky. It was the kind of weather that sucked the joy out of you before the day had even begun. My morning was quite the same. Up at 5:30 a.m., a little bleary-eyed, I set off to coach two treadmill-based classes at Third Space gym in the 'City' location. After coaching both classes I scoffed down breakfast and let the caffeine that I'd swiftly consumed course through my veins. I felt a flicker of determination for what lay ahead. The session was to be brutal, with 20 x 400m sprints and just 60 seconds to catch my breath between each. One word for it: *spicy*. My eyes flickered between the rows of treadmills, choosing the right one like it was a weapon for battle. My carbon-plated speed shoes hugged my feet, promising speed and efficiency – everything I wanted for this session. I felt the buzz of adrenaline bubbling beneath the surface. I pressed start, beginning my warm-up with a light jog as my body readied itself for the mammoth task ahead. Off I went.

Reps blurred into a rhythm of pounding strides, burning lungs and a treadmill hum that grew louder with every nudge up in pace. By the final three reps, my calves began to whisper warnings, sharp and tender in a way that made me grit my teeth. But I pushed the whispers aside. Twenty reps were within reach, and nothing was going to stop me. The final rep came, and I dialled the pace up to a punchy 16kmph. My feet pounded against the belt, each strike vibrating up through my legs. My breathing turned shallow and erratic, but I was locked in. Eyes fixed on the distance counter, I fed myself cues: *Run taller. Fast feet. Push the tread away.* The last 100 metres were a battle in my mind: *Hold on. Yes, you can. Finish strong.* When the screen finally flashed 400m, I let out a shaky exhale and collapsed against the treadmill's handles. My heart hammered at 190bpm; my breath staggered like it might never reset again. Sweat dripped into my eyes, stinging, but I was grinning – a grin of exhaustion, pride and sheer defiance of every doubt I'd had before starting. *Nailed it.* But as I stepped gingerly off the treadmill, the whispers in my calves grew louder, sharper. I brushed it off, convinced it was just the product of a hard-fought session. That night, as I stretched out on the couch, I felt a dull throb in my right calf but shook it off with the same stubborn confidence: *You're fine. Rest and you'll bounce back.*

The next morning, the reality of my body's betrayal hit me like a slap. I swung my legs over the bed and placed my feet on the floor, and a stabbing pain shot through my right calf. I winced, my breath caught in my throat. Each step felt like someone was jabbing a needle into my calf – sharp, jarring, impossible to ignore. My stomach sank. *Rest. Just rest*, I told myself, willing the fear out of my head. I limped through my morning as I taught another double treadmill session. By the last class, walking was a chore. Every step sent a warning shot up my leg. I was so fortunate that Third Space had physios on site, so I hobbled to one, desperate for reassurance. He said he would flush out the calf lightly and it was hopefully nothing to worry about. *Hopefully.* As he massaged my calf, his hands pressing through painful muscles, I gritted my teeth thinking: *this does hurt quite a bit, but surely it's good? This will fix it.*

But it didn't.

The next day, my calf was swollen with ominous yellow bruising. The pain was sharper now – no longer a whisper but a scream. My stomach churned as the truth set in. This wasn't something rest alone could fix. I called my usual physio and booked an emergency appointment, dread knotting in my chest.

His words were a blow. 'You've torn your calf. And not a small tear.'

My thoughts spun. Anger at myself rose within me and continued to build, like my speed had on that treadmill. *Why didn't I stop? Why didn't I listen to my body? Why did I get that massage and make it worse?* The anger burned briefly before inviting fear to the party.

'How long?' I asked, my voice attempting some sort of hopeful wish.

'Best case, if you do the rehab exactly and your body responds well? Four weeks until you're back running. At the earliest.'

Four weeks. I was planning to run the Manchester half-marathon in just seven weeks. The maths was brutal and unforgiving. If I had any chance of running it, there was no chance it would be what I'd dreamed of. My training had been going *so* well. I was stronger, faster, ready to chase a PB I'd worked so hard for. Now, that dream teetered on whether I'd even be healed enough to run. That day, I left the physio with a new companion — not just a damning diagnosis but uncertainty. *Would I recover in time? Would I lose all the fitness I'd worked for? Could I even trust my body again?* Each question sat heavy, unanswered, as I limped home, anger and fear swirling together in a storm I had to face.

Over those seven weeks, I did every single thing my physio told me. I didn't run. I strengthened, I iced, I followed everything to a tee like an A* student. Some days I felt like I could jump on the treadmill and run for miles. Others, just holding the static calf raises I needed to do for forty-five seconds felt like my leg was going to disintegrate beneath me. It was a mixing bowl of emotions, especially while having to do it alongside teaching classes and demoing for them as well. Every day, I got to coach and see others do what I'd give *anything* to be able to participate in. I was proud of them but jealous too. I praised them for each minute of gruelling work they overcame but secretly wished I could be in that breathless discomfort with them.

After five weeks, I'd received my physio's sign-off to run, and I'd never been more excited to get outside. Putting on my runners again felt like coming home. But alongside the joy, an unsteady, apprehensive feeling rose within me. *Could*

I run again? Emma, are you sure it feels ready? Did that step hurt or am I just overthinking it? How do I run again? Is that a twinge? Each step I took, I was on alert to every inch of my body providing feedback. I felt like a child learning to walk — overly aware and completely unsure of my rhythm. The run was not exciting in the slightest. But I did it. I completed 5km after five weeks of continual rehab — hallelujah. However, the light started to dim when I realized that I'd only *just* successfully completed 5km. To add a whole 16km to that in less than two weeks? *Not. Happening.* I begrudgingly DNS (did not start) the Manchester half. My ego took a hit more than anything, but I knew I was making the right choice for future me. It took me a few months to fully recover from that calf tear and to trust not only my legs again, but my ability to run a little faster like I had in those 400m intervals. When your body 'fails' you, that trust and strength need to be rebuilt over time. The trust was reclaimed.

There's no denying that being injured rocks you to your core. For me, it was something I had experienced many times over the years, ever since I was a child. I was fast and grew quickly, so my limbs and co-ordination always took a bit to catch up with each other. An injury was never too far away through my youthful clumsiness.

There was the time I insisted on hanging on to the gate for as long as possible to wind up my dad when I was two. He tried to pull me away, but my hand wanted to stay attached to the gate. One dislocated elbow served right up.

Then there was the time I was seven and had just consumed a sticky ice lolly at my grandma's house. If you gave me sugar

105

at that age, it was like pouring alcohol on a flame. Mum had asked me to clean my hands before I touched anything, so I sprinted to the bathroom, slipped on the mat, flew into the air and landed on my coccyx. A shriek left my throat as I bawled my eyes out. I'd managed to badly bruise my tail-bone and couldn't walk at all for weeks without pain.

Then there was the time before my first holy communion when I was racing our neighbours on my bike. Unknowingly, I slammed on the brakes as we came to the end of the road, squeezed the front brake a fraction before the right and flew over the handlebars, cutting my chin and injuring my jaw. Of course, it was the night before my holy communion when I needed to look darling, yet I had a massive scar on my chin and a swollen jaw. My mum was delighted.

Many of these injuries were a part of childhood reckless-ness – tripping, falling and just general kids' play. Back then, I was mentally resilient. I knew I'd bounce back, but was always frustrated by having to slow down or rest. Still, I was younger, so the recovery was much quicker.

During my early university years, my relationship with in-juries was intertwined with constant soreness. To give context to the level I was exercising at: I trained in netball four times a week, including matches, plus six days a week for athletics, including conditioning or competing on the weekends. Did I explain the true training load to either of my coaches? Nope. Did I expect my body to just keep going? Oh, absolutely. I battled through shin splints, grade-two ankle sprains, thumb and wrist sprains, and Achilles tendinopathy, and in my second year, I was hospitalized for a grumbling appendix (luckily, it did not require surgery). I put my body through it. When injuries stopped me physically, like the grade-two ankle sprains, I showed up and trained my upper body instead. I didn't have an off switch. I'm not about to dictate to you how you should or shouldn't push your body, but what I can say is that listening to mine *truly* helped me distinguish between training that was necessary and training that punished my body.

With this conversation, I have to speak about my mental health. My way of coping during some of my hardest times was through training. My constant need to train and push my body to its limits then, was a coping mechanism to avoid facing the reality of my life during those years. Hiding behind the desire to 'better myself and be the best' was part of my facade of being okay, but exercise became a crutch I used to shut out my mental anguish. Training meant I spent time with people, that I could focus on anything other than the fact that I was nineteen, had just lost my dad to cancer and was feeling broken inside. Without those times in my day to move and exercise with others, I had to confront and process all the grief, trauma and emotions I was feeling. Clearly, I wasn't sufficiently ready to face those hard emotions or to seek help, so I kept going with my training even in the face of the potential for poor consequences.

Let the Challenges Commence

Speaking of pushing myself past my limits, in 2016, I took on one of my craziest challenges ever: 24 hours of burpees. I undertook this challenge to raise money for a cancer charity in honour of my dad. When loved ones suffer from cancer and are battling to survive, they don't have a choice to stop or say, 'I don't fancy having cancer today'. I chose one full day as the time frame for my challenge to reflect this. The reason I selected burpees (a combination of a press-up and a leap into the air) is because they're known as one of the most challenging bodyweight movements in exercise to perform repetitively. The constant battle of having to jump with my own bodyweight, to pick myself back up on repeat, no matter how fatigued I was, felt symbolic of the fight that those with cancer endure.

At the time, I was working at Nike and didn't want to take time off for myself. My first challenge was finding a location close to work, so I could start the challenge at the end of my shift. I located a 24-hour gym near Angel, Islington, and set up to begin at 6 p.m. I wore my Mizuno trainers, simple black leggings, my Cancer Research vest and my gloves for hand protection. From the research I had done, I knew that people's hands could get injured, so I decided to wear combat-style gloves, even though I hadn't worn them before. Rookie error. Wearing the gloves meant my skin had something to rub against with every rep, and as time went on my hands became covered in blisters.

I'd trained by completing over six hours of burpees in one go and had come up with a strategy. I took every hour and broke it into ten-minute sections. I set a number to conquer in that time frame. My goal at the start was to hit one hundred in ten minutes. If I hit one hundred in eight minutes, I gave myself two minutes to drink and eat before starting again for the next ten minutes. For fuel, I relied on jam sandwiches on white bread, for fast-acting sugars, and ready-salted crisps. The crisps and salt were vital, as I'd read some crazy stats about people losing their eye movement from the long endurance element because all their salts had been depleted. I was adamant I wouldn't be joining that club.

The night shift, even with my plan in place, was the hardest. I felt like I was deep in jet lag and slightly delirious as I chipped away during the early hours. At around 3.30 a.m., I took a thirty-minute nap. To this day, I can tell you it was the best nap I've ever had in my life. I got up post-sleep feeling like I'd had a new injection of life. At the twelve-hour mark, I was only doing fifty burpees in ten minutes as my body began to break down. Strategy was everything now. The goalposts had changed, but the pattern remained. If I did fifty reps in seven minutes, I rested the remainder. Instead of seeing twelve hours left, I just focused on the next ten-minute segment and tackling it a rep at a time. Lauren, a good friend of mine, jumped at the chance to crew me and guide me through this mad challenge. She was on a clicker, counting every single rep. My girl was the real MVP that day. When I slept, she did; when I jumped, she clicked.

As the sun rose, and the hours of the morning drifted into

lunch, more friends came to support me, bringing energy and love. Still, I chipped away, ten minutes at a time. Eating, fuelling, resting, again and again and again. With four hours to go, my left foot and right hip were really screaming at me.

At hour twenty-one, I started to feel a strange stabbing in my left foot. Every time I jumped my legs back, it felt like I was standing on a sharp pebble on the beach. At my next rest point, I sat down and palpated my foot. It screamed back as I tried to assess what the damage was. I had two options in this moment: quit and not complete the final three hours – but look after myself and put my body and its needs first – or carry on and complete as many reps as I could to the full twenty-four hours and then deal with the consequences later. I think you can guess the option I chose.

Seven thousand and fifteen.

That's the number of burpees I completed in those 24 hours back in August 2016. At the time, I was the youngest of five people to ever attempt it. As competitive as I am with myself, there is no way I'd do it again or recommend it to a friend. After I finished, I devoured a huge burger and chips before hobbling down to A&E, bringing some hilarity to the doctors and nurses at St George's that evening. 'You did *what* for how long?' After triage and some uncomfortable positions on the x-ray machine, two small black lines appeared on the screen. I had managed to break not one but two metatarsals in my left foot, the fourth and fifth to be precise. I'm not sure what hurt worse after that event: my whole body from the insane DOMs (delayed onset muscle soreness) I had or my foot throbbing in my new best pal, the air boot.

The positive of the burpee challenge was that my mental resilience was unparalleled. Neither fatigue nor injury held me back. On the flip side, the competitive need for completion and pushing through literal broken bones is not something I wish to repeat or would recommend to others. This 24-hour challenge pushed me to places I didn't know I could reach mentally. Places I had to dig deep within my soul to find to keep moving. I was so relieved when it was over and was ready to put my feet up from challenges — at least for a short while.

When I was going through my toughest mental battles, running pulled me out of my all-consuming feelings. I actively sought exercise as my help, as my refuge, and many times crossed a line with my training. With a background in athletics and high-level sport, training six times a week was the norm in school and university. These sessions were guided by a coach, so the intensity was managed to a degree, but once I left university, I was the one in charge. I threw myself into six to seven high-intensity training sessions a week and glorified double days of highly intense training, wearing them like a medal.

At the end of 2017, I pushed my own limit with overtraining, this time leading to my most serious injury. The one that has since changed me for good.

It was a dark winter morning and I was woken up by my 5 a.m. alarm, a time of day I'd seen *way* too often in my life. The priority of getting my training session in before I headed for a full day of clients at Profeet, the running lab I worked at, spurred me on. I got out of bed and was hit with a searing, sharp pain in my hip. Not a little discomfort at all — agony. A solid ten out of ten. Having had experience with dislocations and broken bones, I knew this pain was serious and something was *very* wrong. I attempted to walk, but the pain was blinding. I dropped back into my bed. Luckily, I had some leftover painkillers on my bedside table from shoulder injuries in the past. As I gulped them down, all I could think was, *I've done this to myself*. I had been working with a coach — Joslyn Thompson Rule. Back then, she was a Nike Trainer and someone I looked up to in the industry to help me curb my overtraining habits. But even though I was working with her and completing the sessions Jos gave me, I wasn't completely honest about the amount of training I was doing. I wasn't telling her about the extra Barry's classes, the extra boxing sessions and cheeky runs I was squeezing in after work. The body keeps the score, they say, and I'll never forget that moment lying there in pain, waiting for the tablets to kick in. The score was apparent — I'd lost.

I managed to move my body and get to work and do my job, the tablets keeping me functional. I had booked an emergency appointment for the next day to assess the damage with Rebecca, an osteopath. Becs, as I knew her, had guided me through many near misses of serious injury. She'd been there to untangle and dig through every knot I'd put into my muscles over the years. She knew my body so well, even better than I did. One of the most frustrating parts of this pain was that it had been weeks since I'd seen her. Life had been 'lifeing' and I had neglected my own wellbeing. I'd seen the amber light turn to red and just decided to accelerate anyway. After multiple screenings and tests, a conclusion was made: I had a tear in my labrum. The labrum is the cartilage ring that surrounds the socket of your hip. It's why the pain was so excruciating with every step. 'Devastated' doesn't describe how low I felt from the diagnosis. The walls of my world were closing in, and light was disappearing. I knew this injury could require surgery. I knew this injury could stop people from ever moving pain-free again. This was no joke, and I had done this to myself.

Becs and Jos combined their extensive sports therapy knowledge and put together a plan, one that would keep me away from surgery and help me regain my ability to walk and run pain-free. I promised myself and everyone I engaged with about running and fitness that this was *never* happening again. I was never again going to knowingly overtrain and cause damage to my body. I was never again going to constantly train to shut out my own thoughts and in turn, stop my ability to move and run. Those weeks and months following the injury were extremely hard. It was the depths of winter in the UK, when running usually helped me, and without it, it was tough. Controlling the things I could became my reality. My rehab routine was my downtime and headspace. The constant thought process was: *If I rehab well, I can run again and do it pain-free.* It was the hope I clung to through every boring stretch session, every isometric hold, every moment where I had to resist the urge to push too hard, too soon. There were days when frustration took over, when the finish line felt impossibly far away, but there were also the voices, steady, firm and unwavering, of Jos and Becs confirming it would be okay when I was able to run a little further, lift a

113

little heavier week by week. They knew better than I did in that moment. Jos would often say, 'Emma, you are exactly where you need to be.' Injury forces you to check in with yourself. It stops your ability to move through an emotion and forces you to actually feel it. It reminded me that strength is found not in doing the most, but in the patience of waiting and letting my body heal.

And they were right.

In April 2018, I stood on the starting line of the London Marathon, a different person from the one who had hobbled into Rebecca's office months before. This time, I wasn't just running on adrenaline or stubbornness. I was running on strength, on a body that had been rebuilt with care and discipline. I was running because the privilege of doing so had been taken from me for so long. The marathon was a celebration of that. Hours later, as I crossed the finish line, the roar of the crowd around me felt distant compared to the voice in my head. It wasn't just triumph I felt, it was gratitude. Gratitude for the people who had guided me, for the lessons my injury had taught me and for my own determination to see this through. I had done it. Pain-free. Healthy. Happy. That moment wasn't just about crossing a marathon finish line. It was about reclaiming myself, piece by piece, mile by mile.

This injury, like every other pause I've been forced to take from running, made me realize what a gift running is. That it isn't a given, and one day, I won't always be able to get out and do it. That with the help of others, I owe it to myself to be as strong and as resilient as I can be to keep running for as long as my body allows me to. Overcoming this injury forced me to reconnect, physically, mentally and emotionally. It was a defining moment for me, realizing that exercise is not a tool to shut out my emotions. It's one that enables me to be my best self and work through those thoughts and feelings. Running led me towards healing the relationship I had with myself, through patching up the damage I had done to my body.

If you're just starting this journey of running and learning more about your body, my biggest advice is that small daily changes make all the difference. Check in with your body; listen to the little issues that you might otherwise sweep under the rug as 'adapting to running'. Seek help and advice early on, whether from friends or medical professionals. Looking after the body involves more than just taking rest days. If you have a busy home life, you might be wondering how to find rest. It could be as simple as carving out time in the day for yourself: a thirty-minute bath, a ten-minute stretch in your room with the door closed for some peace. Make space for yourself because you deserve it. There is no rush to be making personal bests. There is no rush to conquer that 5k or 10k. Ensure both your body and mind stay well and on your own path. This is your journey.

FINDING CHALLENGE

When I feel I can't achieve something, I ask myself, *why? What is stopping me? Is it an external reason? Or is it the beliefs I hold about myself?* While navigating my way out of grief and using running to help me, I realized that my mindset was one of the few things I could control. I had the power to become unstuck. I had the power to make the change. I had the power to run. This realization – that I had choices, and I could challenge myself in a healthy way – made my desire to take on physical challenges a big part of my navigating life after Dad's passing. The challenges were a choice to tackle something difficult, not only to better myself but also to raise awareness and money to help better the lives of others.

Before writing this chapter, I asked various people for their definition of a challenge. Phrases that arose included: 'something difficult', 'a big feat' and 'something that altered someone's day to day'. My favourite response came from my four-year-old niece: 'something really, really, really, really, really hard.' A challenge encompasses all of these things and more. In your life, a challenge may simply be carving out the time to run and get started. Whether it's the overwhelm of work or family commitments limiting your training time, challenges come up every single day, no matter how big or small.

Think of your life and the challenges you face that may be simply blocking your ability to run or train for yourself. These could be time constraints, responsibilities, or mental or physical barriers within yourself. Write them down, however many there may be. Once written, look at them and ask yourself: is the challenge in your way achievable? Can you find a way to work around it or even with it? These answers may not come to you right away. But even naming things you find difficult, especially when it comes to running and movement, is a great step to conquering your mind and being solution-driven. That's one of the first steps to overcoming daily challenges you may face.

The challenges that I've battled have always been more mental than physical. Digging deep into your core to find out *why* something feels hard can often be the real work. Is it the physical fitness you need to build? Or is it the mental resilience that you struggle with? What is your main battle? With running, your biggest challenge may be conquering that first 5k. Overwhelm, fear and lack of self-belief may be the core emotions that arise for you. But remember, any and every distance you look to achieve can be built up to. You don't have to tackle the challenge immediately without preparing for it both mentally and physically. Training helps to build your self-belief and with the right plan, anyone can do it. The real secret sauce for me is mindset training.

Having a strong mindset is huge in running. The power of your brain can convince you, even before you start, that you can't do it. Our brains are so powerful that by visualizing a goal we wish to achieve, our body can feel as though we've already achieved it.[1] It's something I've managed to hone and continue to develop, in part, by completing the challenges I've undertaken for charity over the last ten years. Don't be fooled; I didn't click my fingers and decide to have a strong mind. I learned how my mind works and how I can best help myself to tackle hard or seemingly impossible situations. Whether it's in running or day-to-day challenges, the tools below can help you. Please note, I'm not professing to be a guru on conquering the mind, but these tools can hopefully get you halfway there.

Therapy and Counselling

This has been one of the greatest and most fulfilling decisions I've ever made for myself. I believe that without therapy and speaking to someone about how my mind works and my life, I wouldn't be in the position I am now – more confident in my skin and accepting of myself. Nor would I have been able to conquer the challenges I've taken on. It's something I always want to talk about openly, as physical and mental health are so connected. People often joke that running is a replacement for therapy, but there is actually some science behind it.

Running triggers the release of the feel-good hormones: endorphins. I like to call them 'endolphins' instead because that's how they make me feel – like dolphins leaping out of the water. There's also something meditative in the continual repetition of steps, which calms your nervous system. Simply carving out time for yourself to run is a form of self-love amid the craziness of life. It creates space for introspection, without the pressure of rushing straight into something else or being distracted. Along with that, some of us also have the opportunity to run in green spaces, which helps reduce stress levels. I hear the phrase 'go and touch grass' on occasion, which is a polite way of saying, 'go and calm the heck down.' Running has the power to do that, which, yes, can be therapeutic.

But here's the thing: running isn't a substitute for therapy; it's a tool. I've found that nothing compares to having someone listen to you and support you with your issues. Therapy allows you to speak with someone who is completely non-judgemental, who has your wellbeing and best interests at heart. They will ask you about yourself, your life and what has brought you to this moment of seeking therapy. Most of the therapy I've done has been person-centred, involving simply talking to my therapist about my life. There are so many types of therapy, and different things work for different people. Therapy is really uncomfortable; it's hard; it's not something you do once and feel amazing. In reality, you do it multiple times, and it's often painful.

I showed up to therapy because none of the pieces of my life felt like they made sense. Therapy feels like doing a jigsaw puzzle. Sometimes you find new pieces. Sometimes pieces of the puzzle you thought fit in, aren't even part of your puzzle. But piece by piece, session by session, those parts can be found with greater clarity, and the puzzle picture becomes easier to complete. It's a process. The jigsaw won't be completed overnight. Pieces get lost or damaged, but eventually, you can find a way to bring them back to the puzzle and help to complete what was missing in the first place. It's in the rebuilding of this puzzle, in strengthening and understanding your mind, that therapy works. Each one of us is completely different, so I can't say one way is best. But if this is something you have or haven't considered, I urge you to look into it further. Counselling and therapy can take many forms, and I'm aware that the cost of this can be an issue. I'm not blind to my privilege of being able to seek this out. Please know that charities and funds exist to help promote access for everyone.

Chunking

The theory of chunking originates from the theory of cognitive load. Simply put, our brains can't process large amounts of information at once, and the constant accumulation of data from our day-to-day lives can become overwhelming. Overwhelm happens regularly for me in daily life, whether it's the Sunday scaries before a huge work week, or just a task that feels particularly daunting. Chunking is the process of breaking down these tasks into smaller, more digestible pieces of work so that, once each part is complete, you conquer the whole task. Chunking can be hugely helpful when training for longer runs or other physical challenges.

My first use of chunking in exercise was when I took on one of my biggest ever challenges that I wrote about earlier: 24 hours of burpees. One of my proudest achievements that day was being able to manage my timings and the workload across each hour. Without chunking, I don't believe I'd have come close to succeeding that day.

I use this technique pretty much every time I run. In long runs, I have two variations of this method to help me conquer the big distances. The first is dictated by the route. I prefer choosing an out-and-back route for anything over twelve miles. This means that I can run to the six-mile point and literally turn around, running back the way I came. This way, I can create quarter milestones and know I'll come back to the same place, making the distance seem much shorter since, by the halfway mark, I'm headed home. The second option is using local landmarks on running routes. When I run through central London, I utilize my knowledge of places along the river. I know that Canary Wharf to Tower Bridge is 5km. I know that from Tower Bridge up to Big Ben is roughly 6km extra. These benchmarks help me tick off the distance and feel a sense of achievement.

In marathon races, my mathematical brain comes into its own. I always take the first three miles slow and take my first gel (a fast-acting sugary liquid to fuel my body over the miles ahead) at the three-mile mark. I then play a mathematical game and break up the run into three-mile markers and at every one I have a gel. In the race, I look to take on seven to eight gels, so by counting them down, I use the chunking method in a different way to conquer the run.

It doesn't always have to be the longest runs either. When doing speed work, I break up my 400m intervals to make them more manageable. For example, the first 100m is the warm-up into the run, the next 100m I pick the pace to be able to run strong and it gets me to halfway, the next 100m sustains that pace, then the final 100m I accelerate to the finish. Conquering small and achievable portions helps make any event and distance manageable.

Positive Self-Talk/Words of Affirmation

Words have power – the power to cause positive change, but also to keep you stuck. Have you ever had a disagreement with someone and clung on to one line or word they've said? It may have been in the heat of the moment or even in the middle of a whole sequence of positive things they said about you, yet your mind remembers the negative. In running, the way you speak to yourself before, during and after the run has the power to change how you view the whole experience. A mantra that I say daily is: *I can do hard things*. It's a phrase I repeat during key points of a race, but also in my daily struggles to get out the door. For those who have taken on any distance, there is a character-building moment around three quarters of the way through a run where the conflicted self-talk can emerge.

While training for a recent marathon, I programmed myself a 5km time trial – this is a test to see where my best pace and speed were over the distance. I was apprehensive and *really* didn't want to do it. The fear of discomfort is never nice, no matter how much you do it. It took a lot of energy to just make it out the door. In that moment, I used my first tool for mind-shifting self-talk: *I get to*. So many of us forget what a privilege it is to do something, no matter how uncomfortable. Injury is a prime example of taking simple runs for granted. Changing the narrative in my mind for this run to *I get to test myself today* or *I get to see what I'm capable of* is a far more empowering conversation to have.

I started running, but my mind didn't stay positive. Three to four kilometres in, I had the loudest negative voice in my head that wouldn't go away. *Look at your pace. That's not fast enough; you may as well quit now. You're exhausted. Just stop. You're a running coach – you're meant to be better than this. You're so unfit right now, you can't push this.* As mean and intrusive as those thoughts were that day, I didn't let them win. I completed the 5k. What was wild to me was that the negativity of these thoughts lingered. I was extremely down on myself for the rest of the day, rather than proud of myself for conquering a fast 5k.

Throughout my running journey, the battle to conquer the way I speak to myself has remained and is still there even now. Changing my mindset is something I continue to work on, but with positive self-talk in my day-to-day life, I can start to speak better to myself in difficult situations. I regularly consume content that leans in to affirmations and building positive self-talk. Author and all-round incredible black businesswoman Candice Brathwaite says it best in her book *Manifesto*: 'You don't get what you want, you get who you are.' If who I am is someone who, at any given moment, can speak negatively about my actions, then that dialogue needs to change expeditiously. Through running and taking on these challenges, no matter how big or small, you can change how you speak to yourself.

Does my experience sound familiar to you? Think of a time you found extremely challenging and how you spoke to yourself during it. What could you have changed? How could the language you used have been altered for the better? Here are some phrases that you could adopt when negative self-talk tries to rear its ugly head:

'Yes, I can.'

'I get to . . .'

'You didn't come this far, to just come this far.'

'You've got this.'

'This is what the training was for: show yourself your power.'

I also want to talk about understanding your privilege in moments of difficulty. This closely relates to the notion of *getting* to do something. When you're running, or on a journey towards building distance, or taking on a challenge, remind yourself of the privilege of being in that moment. When I coach, I call it the 'magic moment' – the point where quitting seems like the easy option, but instead you choose to carry on. You remind yourself that many would give a lot to be in your position, able to make a change. You have control over your actions, and those actions are moving you closer to your best self, not just in the running space but in life. A strong mindset and practices built in the gym and on the road in the run, translate into a strong mind in our daily lives.

Seek Failure

Stay with me. I'm going to take a sidestep to one of my other loves in sport, basketball, and talk about Michael Jordan. Michael Jordan is arguably one of the greatest athletes of all time. In his career, he accumulated over 32,292 points, and won two Olympic gold medals and six NBA championships with his team, the Chicago Bulls. Now, he's an incredibly successful businessman with a net worth of $3.5 billion as of 2024. Why am I telling you about all his success? Because, in order for him to achieve success, Michael Jordan failed an insane number of times. He famously said:

'I've missed more than nine thousand shots in my career. I've lost almost three hundred games. Twenty-six times I've been trusted to take the game-winning shot and missed. I've failed over and over and over again in my life. And that is why I succeed.'

I had a goal of achieving a sub-four-hour marathon. In running, especially if you're at the start of your journey, time shouldn't be the main focus. Retrospectively, I put way too much pressure on myself to achieve it. Maybe that was because I thought it made me a 'better' runner or coach, but in reality, it just made me stressed. But in my first ever marathon training block, I was hoping to get a sub-four.

I was shooting for the moon, but also putting in the work to make it happen. As a young coach learning my craft, I wrote my own training plan. I read up on all the tools and training methods so I could best achieve 3:59:59 and the 'best workout' for achieving the time. I'd run 20–30 miles a week; I'd strength train twice a week. I committed to completing every single workout, and I was doing four or five each week. I was about to run my first marathon and was sure I could do it. I finished the Amsterdam Marathon in 4 hours and 15 minutes. At the halfway mark my time was 2:01, and I thought I had paced it well. However, in the last 2km, I felt an aggressive stabbing pain under my ribcage. I couldn't breathe deeply, which was crucial when completing the marathon. I forced myself to the finish line through the pain and went to the medical tent straight away. It turned out that the rounded stressed body position I had run in for the last six miles had caused my rib muscles to spasm, which affected my breathing. The doctor was surprised I'd pushed through to the finish. Though 4:15 wasn't the time I wanted, I was proud I had finished, but I also felt I'd failed my body and myself for finishing the way I had. But I hadn't failed. I'd learned my limits and built a foundation for my next races. I've learned to see each 'failure' as a new lesson to learn.

My mantra for the next marathon and beyond was: *Citius, Altius, Fortius*. It was emblazoned on the gate above our heads as we ran through to the Amsterdam finish line. You may recognize these words as the Olympic motto. As you have come to learn, the Olympic Games was where I first found inspiration to run, to push through hard things. So to see those words and run through them when I was struggling most felt poignant. *Faster, Higher, Stronger*. I knew I was going to come back and run this distance better because I was determined to.

127

I failed more times over eight years to achieve a sub-four-hour marathon. In April 2024, in my hometown marathon, the years of strength, lessons, injury and growth built to that finish line – to that moment: 3 hours 54 minutes and 52 seconds.

What is that goal of yours you keep failing at? It doesn't need to be time. I know this is about running, but it may not even be run-related. What is the lesson that you have learned from this 'failure'? What did you do the last time that didn't work? What can be changed? I need you to hear me when I say, failing the first, second, seventh time is meant to happen. It's part of the process.

When I'm teaching classes, I often say: 'the more you try, the more chance you can fail. The more you can fail, the more you can learn, and the more you learn, the more knowledge of yourself you can glean, and knowledge is power!'

If you try a speed or distance goal and succeed – great. You know there is potential to go further or faster next time. But also, if you try and fail at that goal – great! Through that failure, you can learn. You learn your current limit, where you need to work on improving and that learning is your super-power. Seek failure for continued improvement.

Visualization in Marathons

I don't want to run every day. It could be a race you've been working towards for weeks; it could be a training run or a speed session; it could be an easy run: sometimes you are just not feeling motivated. Here is some advice for next time that happens. If you're in kilometre one and have already convinced yourself you won't achieve your goal for that run, your body and mind will believe it. Research has been carried out on the skill of visualization, where you envision yourself completing a task or action before you have done it.[2] Studies show that honing all of your senses (touch, smell, hearing, sight and taste) and doing a mental rehearsal of crossing that finish line can promote the same neurological stimulus as if you're actually doing it. This powerful tool prepares you to achieve and adds calm to the situation.

In April 2024, I ran four marathons in four weeks in commemoration of the twelve years since my dad's death. Four has been my lucky number ever since I was a child. This challenge felt like a perfect way to honour my dad and raise vital funds for brain tumour research in his name. Week 1 was Brighton Marathon, Week 2 was in Lake Garda, Week 3 was the London Marathon and the final week was a self-led run along the Thames Path.

The first race in Brighton was my A race. This was the race I was gearing up to run my fastest ever marathon. Up to this point, I hadn't run under four hours ever before, as you know. This time round I had a different plan. I started training for these marathons in November 2023. The goal up until the new year was to build strength and decide my intentions for Brighton. *What time could I go for?*

Goal setting is such an important part of taking on a challenge. For 2024, I set the goal of a 1:50 half marathon before April, and I set three goals for marathon day. My gold goal, if I had the perfect running day, was 3:55. My silver goal was sub-four hours, and my bronze goal was a PB, which then was anything less than 4:04. With all my goals in hand, running or otherwise, I got creative and made a vision board. This was something I've actually been doing since I was a teenager, and you may have, too. Did you ever cut images out of magazines to stick on your bedroom wall or make collages of things you aspired to or were inspired by as a child? Well that, my friends, is a vision board.

On mine for 2024, I had many things — one was for this book to be written, another to travel to certain countries around the world, and in the top left-hand corner was the time 3:55. I made the board on a photo-editing software so I could download it to my phone and have it as my screensaver. Then, every day, every time I picked my phone up, I saw my dreams, my goals, and could speak them into existence daily.

Fast forward to race day at the start line as I was controlling my breathing, trying to steady my nerves. I looked at my phone one final time. *I am a 3:55 marathon runner.* As Paula Radcliffe started our race, the gun went off and I settled in to the run, listening to the pace my body wanted to go at for the first two to three miles. When you arrive at the Brighton seafront and turn left from the main roads, you are on rolling hills. The type of hills you only realize you are on once you're running down the other side, praying your quads can hold on. These hills went on for 3 miles out and 3 miles back to the 13-mile marker. My legs were battered after the final hill. *I am a 3:55 marathon runner*. The last 4 miles were the longest of my life. I was fighting with every step to keep my momentum forwards, to chase down my goal time. *I am a 3:55 marathon runner*. In the last 400m, I sprinted towards the line. Well, it felt like a sprint but in reality it was just a slightly faster run. The time? 3:54:52. *I did it.* Of course, the months of training were part of it. Of course, my grit and determination were part of it. But since January, every day I had affirmed and adopted the identity of a 3:55 marathon runner – and that I was. How can you utilize this? Every year, I'll now create a vision board as my screensaver to lean in to what I'm aspiring to achieve that year.

During the London Marathon, I used visualization in a slightly different way. I had been lucky to have run the race twice before, so was familiar with the iconic route. Having run two marathons over the previous two weeks, my legs were heavy on that start line, but I sat in the feeling, a moment of privilege for even being there. As I finished my warm-up, I took a moment of calm and thought about the finish line.

I saw myself running past Buckingham Palace as I turned down the Mall to see the finish line adorned with Union Jacks on either side of the road. The time I had set myself as a goal was on my watch. I could hear the deafening roar of the crowd in my ears, the feel of the road as my stride opened and I powerfully pushed the ground away. I could taste the salty, sugary taste of sweat and my last gel in and around my mouth. I could smell my favourite food post-run (a burger FYI), just after I had felt the beautiful medal put round my neck. Writing this now takes me back to that moment, and it was exactly as I had thought, even down to the post-run burger being demolished, too. This run was one of my most memorable of the four marathons because it was the one I surprised myself with. I achieved a sub-four-hour marathon for only the second time in my life, the first having been two weeks prior. This race was actually the only one I visualized my finish for, and I believe it helped in my achieving it.

Can you visualize achieving your next goal or challenge? Think about what you will see, feel or touch, taste, smell and hear. Write it down exactly as I have, even down to the emotions you anticipate. Then, in the coming weeks and days leading up to the event, recall that finish line with every sensation you've noted.

Along with these tools, my many challenges have changed me for the better. Through my burpee challenge (which I'd never do again), I learned that we unknowingly set our own limits within our comfort zone. It was only when taking on that challenge that I realized how our minds protect us from discomfort. My limits were far greater than I'd initially believed. I was capable of more than I thought.

Now, I'm not saying you should undertake a wild physical challenge to discover your limits. But have you ever set yourself a goal that you later altered because you thought it was impossible? Have you disregarded achieving a parkrun or training for a 10k because your mind couldn't fathom it? My advice: trust yourself. Through running, I've discovered another layer of who I am and built my mental resilience. It has given me purpose, and I'm confident it can help you find yours too.

FINDING YOURSELF

Running has always been a constant thread woven throughout every phase of my life, evolving alongside me and taking on new meaning as I've grown. As a child, running was simple, pure and unburdened, an extension of joy, playfulness and boundless energy. It wasn't about goals or destination, it was about the sheer delight of movement. Back then, running was carefree, an effortless reminder of the joy found in the simplest things. I lost it for a few years, but I'm so happy I found it again.

As I got older and faced deeper challenges, particularly the loss of my dad, my relationship to running transformed. It felt different. It became more than just a physical activity, a lifeline, a tool to help me navigate the heavy emotions and confusion that loss and grief had brought me. In those difficult times, running gave me the space to reconnect with myself when my mind felt chaotic and overwhelming. With every step, I found a sense of grounding, a quiet opportunity to reflect and rebuild parts of myself that felt fragmented. It allowed me to take small, steady strides forwards, both physically and emotionally, giving me room to process grief and begin healing in my own way.

I've realized that running isn't just about exercise or performance for me; it's about creating space, space to think, to feel and to discover who I truly am in my most authentic self. It has become my sanctuary, a place where my thoughts can unfold freely without judgement or interruption. No matter how complex a situation or experience might be, running has never promised to make everything better but it has always offered me something equally important: time. Time to reflect, to take stock of where I am and to understand what matters most.

Whether I'm running to find joy, to heal or simply to escape for a moment, it's been a constant in my life that adapts to meet my needs. Running has helped me process life's highs and lows, and in doing so, it has shaped not just how I move but how I navigate towards my best self. An often unspoken point about running is that it shows you who you really are. It shows you how capable you are. When you run and complete a run, you never regret it. Each run unlocks a lesson to help you progress forwards, whether that is in your self-development or physically. It's why I'm enamoured by it and what it's done for me but also what it can do for you too.

Your story may not follow the same path as mine. Running may have already brought you a lot. Or you may be looking to bring running into your life, to explore it. Just because I ran marathons doesn't mean you must. Your story is yours to discover.

I'm about to go on a run. Not a particularly big one or special one. No race with cheering crowds. It's simply my time to go on an ordinary run, the space in my day that I know will make me feel more me. I look out the window for motivation but the sun is so hidden behind a bleak greyness that you wouldn't even know it existed. I head to my drawers and source the most vibrant kit, and as I put it on, I remember all the runs these clothes have carried me through, the joyous moments this kit has brought me. I find not only comfort in them, but unwavering pride. I sit down to tie the laces on my shoes. The shoes that have run me through 10ks, marathon finish lines and most importantly, days like today when it feels hard.

I peer round the corner of the front door and look up, hoping for a stark contrast to the eleven minutes prior. No change. On the greyest days, I remember that I get to move my body, I get to feel the ground pushing back against me to feed that momentum I've created. With every step, the initial effort I struggled with turns to ease as my heart beats steady and my breathing rate becomes a melodic hum. I step outside, and will continue to step outside or onto that treadmill, because being guided by my mood is not where growth happens. Instead, I am guided by the fact I know this run will change my day, as it has my life. I hope it does the same for you.

PART 2
HOW TO RUN

Taking that step on my first run changed my life. It brought so much power into my world, and now it's time to see what that change could do for you. Whether you already run, have never run a day in your life or have simply picked up this book out of curiosity, the goal is to build more consistency with running. To begin, and so you can have a smooth journey, having the right knowledge and tools is key. So here I am. In this section of the book, I'll try to simplify every quote, piece of advice or 'fact' on running you may have been told. I'll share best practices on how to warm up, avoid injury, stay strong and simply begin.

There will be more focus on data and practical advice alongside my own personal experiences. But even if I get carried away with the science-y knowledge part (which FYI I will — there is so much to learn), it will always come back to why running is important, and how having information and a foundation of knowledge can help you on your own journey. There will be practical running guides, strength workouts with QR codes linking you to instructional videos, advice on key areas of running, interviews with runners sharing their motivations and more.

Are you ready to start and see what running can bring to your life?

FINDING THE START

It's time to start running. Starting doesn't necessarily mean beginning from scratch. Some of you may be reading this having run in the past, but with limited support or intention behind it. When you start this time, I want you to ask yourself: why? Why do you want to run? Is it to have space and time with yourself for your wellbeing? A goal, distance or time you wish to achieve? To try something that scares you? These are all valid motivations.

Motivations can come in two key forms: intrinsic and extrinsic. Intrinsic motivation is doing something because of the feelings it brings. This reasoning is usually deeply personal and emotive, as you have seen from my story. Many of my motivations are this kind of motivation. Are you seeking the freedom, clarity or peace running can bring? Is there a personal drive you have that you want running to fulfil? In contrast, extrinsic motivation comes from doing something in order to earn an external reward. For example, a medal, or a time achieved for a certain distance. It could be as fun as betting with a friend on who can complete the 5k first or the most number of times in a month. This could also be something you are driven to do in order to receive compliments from others. These two types of motivations are used best in conjunction with each other because they combine to create a stronger and more sustainable drive to run. For example:

- You sign up for a marathon to achieve a goal time (extrinsic), but you stick with the training because you love the mental headspace the long runs give and how they show you the power of your mind (intrinsic).
- You sign up with your run group to race a 5k (extrinsic), but you also love the community element of your group and how it makes you feel proud of yourself for running with others (intrinsic).
- You start running to lose weight (extrinsic), but over time realize that running gives you self-belief and happiness (intrinsic) so you keep doing it even once the weight is off.

Being passionate and finding enjoyment in your goals can help to reduce burnout and the likelihood of quitting. Falling in love with the process aids in not only achieving those goals but maintaining your drive well after they have been achieved.

Towards You
Think about your 'why' for running. Write a list of reasons why you want to, or already do, run. Then, as with the three examples above, create three of your own intrinsic and extrinsic motivations.

Now you have your why, let's dive in to how we can start and improve your first steps on your running journey.

Beginner – Start

Starting is the hardest part of running. If you are reading this as your first step into the running world, I've got you. The first myth I want to dispel is that you have to run non-stop throughout a run to be classified as a runner. I believed this to be true for a long time, even when I was consistently running and training. I remember stopping to walk on one run after twenty minutes of running and thinking: *well, that was a waste of time. (Which it most definitely wasn't.)* I believed at the time that if I walked, I couldn't call myself a runner, that I was somehow less worthy in this new sport I was getting into. All of those thoughts about walking during a run are incorrect. A runner is someone who shows up – no matter the weather or the challenge – laces up their shoes and commits to the journey. They embrace the rhythm of their breath and the pounding of their feet, knowing each step is a testament to persistence and inner strength. Through triumphs and setbacks, they find freedom in movement and clarity in the struggle. A runner isn't defined by pace or distance, but by their resilience and the unwavering spirit that keeps them moving forwards, chasing growth, joy and a connection to themselves with every stride. So, lace up those shoes, take yourself outside and let's go for a run.

In the next few pages, I've created a simple and easy-to-follow running plan for you to begin your journey. Over the course of nine weeks, you will continually build up your resilience and strength with the goal of running thirty minutes non-stop. The reason we're using nine weeks is to give you plenty of time to adapt and progressively build stamina – this way, the body can adjust without risking injury. For the timings listed below, you can use a simple stopwatch on your phone to guide you through the runs. Each session will begin with a warm-up, followed by your session, then end with a cool-down.

In Weeks 1–2, you'll repeat the same workout two to three times. Space these sessions out across the week so you always have rest days in between. For example, you might run on Monday, Thursday and Saturday, with the other days as rest from running. Remember, the run isn't about sprinting as fast as you can. We build up our tolerance brick by brick, step by step.

For some, the 'run' portions may begin as a fast walk rather than breaking into a run. Take your time over the first two weeks. If you need to repeat Weeks 1 and 2 a couple of times, please do. It's not a failure. It's the way we learn. We learn our current capacity and we can adapt for the future. If that means this plan becomes twelve weeks because you repeat weeks, or because life gets in the way, or you just want more time to adjust to the run, that is okay. Progress isn't always linear. Forwards is a pace. Take a deep breath and here you go:

Beginner – 9-Week Run Plan

	SESSION 1	SESSION 2	SESSION 3
Week 1	5 min warm-up: brisk walk Main session: 1 min run, 1 min walk – repeat 4 times Cool-down: 5 min walk Total length: **18 min**	5 min warm-up: brisk walk Main session: 1 min run, 1 min walk – repeat 5 times Cool-down: 5 min walk Total length: **20 min**	5 min warm-up: brisk walk Main session: 1 min run, 1 min walk – repeat 6 times Cool-down: 5 min walk Total length: **22 min**
Week 2	5 min warm-up: brisk walk Main session: 1 min run, 1 min walk – repeat 7 times Cool-down: 5 min walk Total length: **24 min**	5 min warm-up: brisk walk Main session: 1 min run, 1 min walk – repeat 8 times Cool-down: 5 min walk Total length: **26 min**	5 min warm-up: brisk walk Main session: 2 min run, 1 min walk – repeat 6 times Cool-down: 5 min walk Total length: **28 min**
Week 3	5 min warm-up: brisk walk Main session: 1 min run, 1 min walk – repeat 10 times Cool-down: 5 min walk Total length: **30 min**	5 min warm-up: brisk walk Main session: 5 min run, 2.5 min walk – repeat 3 times Cool-down: 5 min walk Total length: **32.5 min**	5 min warm-up: brisk walk Main session: 3 min run, 1.5 min walk – repeat 5 times Cool-down: 5 min walk Total length: **32.5 min**

	SESSION 1	SESSION 2	SESSION 3
Week 4	5 min warm-up: brisk walk Main session: 6 min run, 3 min walk, 8 min run, 4 min walk Cool-down: 5 min walk Total length: **31 min**	5 min warm-up: brisk walk Main session: 2 min run, 1 min walk – repeat 8 times Cool-down: 5 min walk Total length: **34 min**	5 min warm-up: brisk walk Main session: 6 min run, 2.5 min walk – repeat 3 times Cool-down: 5 min walk Total length: **35.5 min**
Week 5	5 min warm-up: brisk walk Main session: 2 min run, 3 min walk, 4 min run, 2 min walk, 2 min run Cool-down: 5 min walk Total length: **23 min**	5 min warm-up: brisk walk Main session: 4 min run, 3 min walk – repeat 2 times Cool-down: 5 min walk Total length: **24 min**	5 min warm-up: brisk walk Main session: 15 min run Cool-down: 5 min walk Total length: **25 min**
Week 6	5 min warm-up: brisk walk Main session: 4 min run, 2 min walk, 2 min run, 2 min walk – repeat 2 times Cool-down: 5 min walk Total length: **30 min**	5 min warm-up: brisk walk Main session: 7 min run, 3 min walk, 8 min run Cool-down: 5 min walk Total length: **28 min**	5 min warm-up: brisk walk Main session: 18 min run Cool-down: 5 min walk Total length: **28 min**

	SESSION 1	SESSION 2	SESSION 3
Week 7	5 min warm-up: brisk walk Main session: 5 min run, 1.5 min walk – repeat 4 times Cool-down: 5 min walk Total length: **36 minutes**	5 min warm-up: brisk walk Main session: 8 min run, 3 min walk, 8 min run Cool-down: 5 min walk Total length: **29 minutes**	5 min warm-up: brisk walk Main session: 22 min run Cool-down: 5 min walk Total length: **32 minutes**
Week 8	5 min warm-up: brisk walk Main session: 6 min run, 1.5 min walk – repeat 4 times Cool-down: 5 min walk Total length: **40 min**	5 min warm-up: brisk walk Main session: 10 min run, 3 min walk, 10 min run Cool-down: 5 min walk Total length: **33 min**	5 min warm-up: brisk walk Main session: 25 min run Cool-down: 5 min walk Total length: **35 min**
Week 9	5 min warm-up: brisk walk Main session: 15 min run Cool-down: 5 min walk Total length: **25 min**	5 min warm-up: brisk walk Main session: 20 min run Cool-down: 5 min walk Total length: **30 min**	5 min warm-up: brisk walk Main session: 30 min run Cool-down: 5 min walk Total length: **40 min**

As you work your way through each week, reflect on:
- Three positives you took away from the runs that week.
- One thing you found difficult and can address next week. For example, maybe you struggled to catch your breath at times; remember it's normal and you can always focus on steadying it next week.

Let's also look at some simple tips which can help you to run as efficiently as possible. No matter where you are in your journey, efficiency in your movement is what you want to strive for. The more efficient you are as a runner, the less running will hurt and the faster and further you'll be able to go.

Disclaimer: You're not going to be perfect on run one — maybe not even perfect on run one hundred — but what we're looking for is finding what works best for you and how we can channel that 'best' with every step. Begin by being kind to yourself. None of us were ever taught *how* to run as children. Unless you competed in athletics or ran on the track, the chances are, you've never learned what running 'properly' actually looks like. I was the same.

In the early days when I began tuning into my body, I remember coming back from runs with aches in unexpected places. It felt like my body was keeping score of my inefficiencies. I'd feel tension in my upper body, as though I'd been running down the street with coiled springs in my shoulders and arms. My knees would ache from what felt like absorbing the weight of a baby elephant with every stride. During a run, I'd be out of breath, gasping, like the air was thinning with every kilometre that passed. Now, I can't change these things immediately for you, but I can give you solutions to help you conquer these problems if they rear their heads.

The changes we'll make will improve your running economy. Your running economy is about how efficiently your body is able to utilize oxygen when running at any given pace. This efficiency is dependent on multiple things, such as your body's mechanics, form and your physiological ability, such as your heart rate and breathing rate. I like to use the analogy of a car to describe this. A fuel-efficient car can travel further on less petrol than an inefficient one, so it then costs less to run. The same is true for a runner and their economy. If you're reading this as a beginner, I know it can be overwhelming. If that's the case, you can come back to this at a later stage because right now, going for the run is enough.

The next few pages will be helpful — maybe not right now, but further down the line. As you progress, the last thing I want you doing is wasting the energy you create.

So, let's begin by making your running FETCH. Yes, I truly am trying to make fetch happen (if this millennial joke missed you, please go and watch *Mean Girls*). This acronym is going to help you understand key metrics to dial into when it comes to your running efficiency.

F – Feet Under Your Body

When running, aiming to land your feet directly under your body, not out in front is essential. This is known as running closer to your centre of gravity (COG). Over-striding takes place when you aren't landing with feet under the body, which has been shown to increase force into the knee joints and slow you down.[1] Running closer to your COG helps you to stay balanced, reduces impact on your joints and improves efficiency. Think of your feet pushing the ground away as you run and then pulling your heel up towards your buttocks in the shape of a horizontal teardrop, with each step landing beneath your hips. This prevents over-striding, which, as well as slowing you down, can increase injury risk. Incorporating a slight forwards lean from your ankles as you run will encourage the ideal foot position – i.e. landing directly under your body.

You may be thinking: does foot position matter? By foot position, I'm speaking about which part of your foot makes initial contact with the ground – your heel, midfoot or forefoot. The answer is yes, it does. Striking through the midfoot has been found to be the most efficient foot position and reduces likelihood of injuries. Landing on your midfoot can place your body in a better position to propel yourself forwards and reduce forces being emitted through the lower leg.[2]

Other research has found recreational runners are more likely to heel strike due to over-striding but essentially, the big focus is preventing injury. If landing with your feet under your body still causes you to naturally heel strike, then heel strike away. This is not something to concern yourself with too much as you begin your running journey, and you may find that as you run more, your strike pattern may adapt and change as you become more akin to the motion of running.

E – Engaged Core

Running with a stronger and engaged core helps to maintain posture and reduce the impact going through the lower limbs with every step, and most significantly increases running efficiency and performance.[3]

Firstly, your core isn't just your abdominal region on your stomach. Your core also includes your glutes, lower back and the front of your hips. To engage your core, I want you to think of your hips/pelvic region like a full glass of water. Running without the core engaged will cause your pelvic position to be tilted downwards and result in losing some water from the glass. By tucking your pelvis towards your spine, and lengthening your upper body, the core is now engaged and the glass of water can remain upright.

T – Turnover High

Now your feet are landing underneath your body, let's think about the amount of steps you are taking at any given pace. This is called your cadence. This metric is usually calculated in steps per minute (SPM). Research has found that most new and recreational runners are mostly at 155 SPM, while high-level athletes are at 170, even when running slower. This number can vary depending on your height and pace. If you are running with a low cadence, you can increase your likelihood of injury because taking less steps increases the amount of time you spend on the ground.

Increased contact time = increased stress on muscles/tendons = increased injury risk

An increase in SPM of 5–15 per cent has been associated with fewer knee injuries, reduced impact loads and less muscle damage.[4]

There are many ways to help increase or decrease your cadence to the sweet spot. Firstly, try to identify your current cadence. You can do this with the help of a metronome set to differing beats/steps per minute, or it can be through the use of a running app/watch if you use them, too. Set a minute timer and count how many steps one foot takes in a minute at your easy run pace. Easy pace is one that if you had to rate it out of 10 (where 10 is your hardest effort and 1 a walking effort), it would sit as a 3 or 4. After the minute is over, times that by two – this will give you your cadence. Then use a free metronome app to input your current cadence. Over time, increase the cadence by 5 per cent and run on it using the beat of the metronome. If your first figure for cadence sits outside the suggested ranges, don't panic. It's not the end of the world. You're not a bad runner. You're just learning about these things, and that's why I'm here to help.

Small changes can be made to improve it over time and keep you injury free and the most efficient runner you can be.

To begin, if you like listening to music, try running and listening to a drum and bass playlist (I've linked mine below on the QR code). Drum and bass music on average, sits at around 170-176 BPM (which is the same as SPM in running). Simply play the tracks and notice if you naturally run on the beat or not. If you find it very difficult to keep up, then searching for a lower cadence to begin with, maybe a 160–170 BPM playlist, will be more beneficial.

Next, run on a treadmill while you make these changes. Cadence is a strange concept to dial into initially. A very common response to making a change is to end up running faster. You want to turn the feet over quicker but hold the same pace. A treadmill is the greatest facilitator for this. Set your pace and start to play with changing the amount of steps you take. You may find yourself getting out of breath initially while you adjust to the new form. Be kind to yourself and build it in slowly.

C – Chest Proud and Lean

Running with your chest proud will encourage you to run taller. The action of running taller will help you to run with your feet under you, slightly lean forwards, engage that core and allow gravity to help you take on that next step.

H – Hands and Arms Relaxed

Keeping your hands relaxed when running has a knock-on effect as it keeps your arms relaxed and your shoulders away from your ears. This relaxed state will enable you to utilize the arm drive you are performing when running. Arm drive is the pumping back and forth of the fists and elbows to generate power in your legs. Have you ever been aware of your arms driving in front of you and across your body when you run? When this happens, the energy you are creating is increasing your rotational movement and reducing the force going into actually moving forwards. A favourite phrase of mine during a run class or track session is 'the arms drive the legs when the legs don't want to go'. Whether you are sitting or standing right now, power your arms like you're running. What do you notice? Your hips are moving, aren't they? The more power and intention you put into your arm drive, the more your hips will move and so power your legs. Drive your hands from 'hips to nips'. This catchy and memorable phrase will help you move those arms more efficiently than ever. Arms that drive further than this range can become inefficient to the runner and may create other injury issues.

Now you know the best way to start, and the form that will enable you to be your best, let's address the toolkit you will need. I say need. The magic of running is that you can simply get out an old pair of shoes, go out and run. You don't *need* anything fancy. To get outside and run you don't need the latest kit or hundreds of different matching sets of clothes. This toolkit offers suggestions of things that can be of great use to help you run more comfortably and stay on track. Even now, I have days where I wake up and don't want to run. If anything, I have more days like that than the days I wake up and do want to go. The mindset shift I use in these times is realizing what I *get* to do, returning to my why, and that helps me drag myself out of bed and hit the road. Here are some additional great tools you can adopt to keep you on track as you start your journey.

The Beginner Runner's Toolkit:

HAVE AN ACCOUNTABILITY PARTNER

This doesn't necessarily need to be someone who runs with you, although that would be great. But see if there is someone in your life who will check in with you to see if you are keeping up with the plan, if you moved your body. Now of course, there are occasions where a run seems impossible. Perhaps you're fatigued or it has been a busy week. Skipping a run is *absolutely* fair and valid. You don't have to beat yourself up for it – that day, it may be the best thing for you.

KNOWING WHERE YOU ARE IN YOUR MENSTRUAL CYCLE

Knowledge is power. When it comes to the menstrual cycle, understanding the impact it has on the mind and body is important and, for many, can be validating. Being able to support yourself, or those people in your life who have periods, with this knowledge and understanding of how the body works is empowering.

The menstrual cycle can be anywhere from twenty-one to thirty-five days, with the most common being twenty-eight days, and it has four distinct phases: menstruation, the follicular phase, ovulation and the luteal phase. The end of the luteal phase can be the most rife with premenstrual symptoms, known as PMS. Mood changes, energy dips and poor sleep are just a small handful of the many symptoms people suffer from. For runners who have a menstrual cycle, it can be challenging to exercise throughout this time. For some, they may have zero symptoms or have worse symptoms during their period or ovulation. Knowing where you are in your cycle, your body's symptom patterns, mood and inclination to train can be very important.

I'm no doctor, but a great friend of mine is. A pioneering one at that, who has researched and championed women's health throughout her career. Dr Hazel Wallace's work in her first book, *The Female Factor*, is a great starting point to help

154

you understand your body. Then *Not Just a Period* dives further into learning about seven key aspects of women's health: nutrition, movement, sleep, mood, libido, body image, skin and hair, examined for the first time through the eyes of the menstrual cycle. It's a joy to see that, now, there is such a broad-reaching conversation about women's health and the effect of the menstrual cycle on exercise; there are so many incredible tools and research you can seek online to continue your own understanding.

RUNNING KIT IS ESSENTIAL

Having a kit that works specifically for you and how you move makes all the difference to your running. If you're reading this and just starting out, I know the running shoe and clothing market is expensive. My advice here is purely guidance, and remember: brands have sales, there are older models of shoes and kit, and there are charity shops that will have lots of kit, as well as friends and family. It all still works. Contrary to what social media tells you, it's *absolutely* okay to not have the latest shiny, bright model.

Tops/Leggings

The key thing here is that the clothing is made from breathable, moisture-wicking material. Most of these materials are made out of polyester. Cotton tops and bottoms will not only cause overheating and discomfort but also can make you more prone to chafing/rubbing of your skin. The length of top/bottoms is personal to each of you, and there are also many options of hijabs made for sports too. The progress we love to see.

Sports Bra

This could be a whole chapter in itself, as having the correct sports bra can revolutionize your running experience. Unsurprisingly, research found that breasts were a physical barrier to exercise for 17 per cent of women.[5] Breast pain and poor support are two of the biggest causes of discomfort in running.

Joanna Wakefield-Scurr, also known as the 'bra professor', has studied the area of breasts and breast movement for decades, completing in-depth research on how they move during exercise and how to support them. One study carried out at the University of Portsmouth, which Joanna shared in *The Times*, stated, 'In our lab, when women are exercising without wearing a bra, we've seen up to 21cm of movement.'[6] There's not only damage from not wearing a bra; the effect on the body from incorrect bras for running can be huge.

From back pain to breast pain, increased rotational forces and excess arm movement, having a correctly fitting sports bra is really important. Due to ill-fitting sports bras, I have scars on my back and under my breasts from chafing night-mares. Post-run showers after bra chafe are ingrained in my memories. I don't want that for you, so I have had the pleasure of learning from Dr Wakefield-Surr, and her research suggests focusing on four key areas when it comes to the fit of your sports bra:

- Band tightness around the ribs. You want a firm fit that is not too restrictive, with minimal give to the band so it hugs the ribcage well.
- Ensure all breast tissue is within the cup of the bra. If there are wrinkles or gaps in the fabric, the cup is too big. On the other hand, if your breasts are spilling out, it's likely too small.
- Make sure the shoulder straps are not overly loose or digging in. You want to have two fingers of give between the strap and shoulder.
- Lastly, the classic jump test: are you supported when jumping in the bra?

The most supportive bras out there on the market are known as encapsulation bras. They combine compression of the breast tissue with separation of the breasts to be held well. A high-impact bra is recommended for running, no matter your cup size.

Socks
I said it once but I'll say it again, cotton is not a friend of yours when it comes to workout apparel. Cotton socks can increase your risk of blisters, because they absorb and hold on to moisture from your sweat. When your feet get damp, any friction between your foot, the sock and your shoe can irritate the skin. Over time, this repeated rubbing damages the top layer of skin – leading to blisters.

To prevent this, use socks made with synthetic materials to help the foot breathe. There are many great brands offering running-specific socks, so seek them out. Take note, some offer dual-layer socks, where one layer holds your foot and the other layer allows friction with the shoe. This initially sounds great. But for some, the layers will increase heat in the foot which can create a breeding ground for moisture. Try to test a range of different sock types and brands to find the best option for you.

Running Shoes

After sports bras, if you need them, these are the most import-ant item you purchase. You don't need the most expensive, top-of-the-range shoe to start. You need something comfort-able. There is research that argues that basing shoe choice on comfort alone is a great place to start. This is known as the comfort filter.[7]

Does that mean second-hand shoes are an option if you want to keep the cost down? Yes and no. If they are pretty much brand new or have one or two wears in them, then go for it. But beware of shoes which have been heavily used. When running becomes a bigger part of your life (just you wait), you will want to consider a brand-new, more technical shoe. I like to use the analogy of glasses. You wouldn't pick up the same glasses your friend has and expect them to be the perfect prescription for you. You'd expect to get your eyes checked, have the lenses adjusted for you and then choose your frames. Running shoes are the same. Gait analysis is the method by which shoes can be given to you based on your body's movement and function. In a later chapter, I'll delve further into shoe choice and feet.

Lay Your Kit Out the Night/Morning Before
As someone who prefers running in the morning, putting the least amount of barriers in my way to get out the door is paramount. Laying out my kit the night before enables me to remove the excuse of searching for my kit to get out the door. Try it and see if it makes your routine smoother!

I hope this chapter has given you the tools to get started and the knowledge to keep improving your runs each time you go out. The run plan is there to guide you. Remember, if one week it feels too much or too hard, scale back and repeat the previous week. That's not a failure — it's adaptation.

In my early days of running, simply starting runs was the hardest part. But remembering my 'why', that I wanted to overcome depression and improve my mental health, made me keep going. Remember your why. My top tips (FETCH) are there to help you, not to overwhelm you. I highly advise focusing on just one of these per run. Stick with, for example, placing your feet under hips for the first 1–2 weeks. Once you feel confident in that, move on to the next tip. Even writing this as someone who has been running for years, I continue to refer back to FETCH. I'm not perfect and neither will you be. That's okay. Remove the pressure to be the best and congratulate yourself for being out there. For beginning. For taking these first steps.

KEY TAKEAWAYS:

- Starting slow isn't a setback — it's smart.
- Form matters more than speed. Using the FETCH method (Feet, Engage core, Turnover, Chest proud, Hands relaxed) helps improve running efficiency, reduces injury risk and builds long-term strength.
- Cadence is your rhythm. Improving your steps per minute (using tools like a metronome or drum & bass playlist) can significantly improve your running economy and reduce injury risk.
- Kit is about comfort, not cost. You don't need the latest gear. Focus on breathable materials, proper support (especially sports bras), moisture-wicking socks and comfortable, functional shoes.
- Progress isn't linear — but forwards is a pace. Your journey is your own. Repeating weeks, adjusting your pace or taking rest days aren't failures — they're part of sustainable growth.

FINDING THE SCIENCE OF RUNNING

It's time for my scientific specs to go on as I take you into my favourite part of running. Now before we start, there is no 'right' way to run that everybody should do. Everybody is different with different bone sizes, different foot shapes, different muscle sizes and strengths. How can I tell you one specific way to run when we are all so unique? This is where learning about the science of running matters. Understanding your own movement and mechanics will arm you with the tools to take on advice that works for you and to understand that it's not a one-size-fits-all approach when it comes to running and biomechanics.

This chapter will have some very specific terminology that you may not have come across before, so I've included simplistic descriptions and some diagrams to illustrate. If you are a very new beginner and this feels overwhelming, don't worry about it for the moment — it is guidance to help you develop your running practice. As ever, the most key thing you need to do to run? Get outside and run. But for now, let's dive into the science to help you discover and understand how you run.

From the age of fourteen, I saw this individuality, that we all have unique bodies, when I was working in my first-ever Saturday job at the Jog Shop in Brighton. It was here I learned my very first pieces of knowledge about footwear and bio-mechanics. The shop was established in 1986, when Sam Lambourne, a prolific runner himself (with an impressive 2:18 marathon time) wanted to offer runners access to specialist running footwear. At the time, it was difficult to source shoes with half and full sizes to try on, and Sam saw a space for that. Through my time working at the shop, I learned how to look for differing foot shapes and align these shapes to different brands. For example, historically, feet with a narrow heel, wider forefoot and high arch profile would work well with the brand Mizuno. New Balance were one of the early brands to offer width fittings, so if a client had super narrow or super wide feet, they were my go-to. I learned that the key to understanding a runner's movement is to start with their foot shape and their mechanics of movement. When we run, our feet are the first point of contact to the ground. If our feet aren't functioning correctly, then it can be a key source to any and every issue and injury related to running that we may develop.

The Different Types of Feet and Why You Need to Know This

Feet are the blueprint to a runner's makeup and after this chapter, you'll hopefully see why. If you know how and what your feet do, you can be best informed when not only looking for footwear, but also when it comes to understanding your strengths and weaknesses.

Let's look at the breakdown of a standard foot and its anatomy.

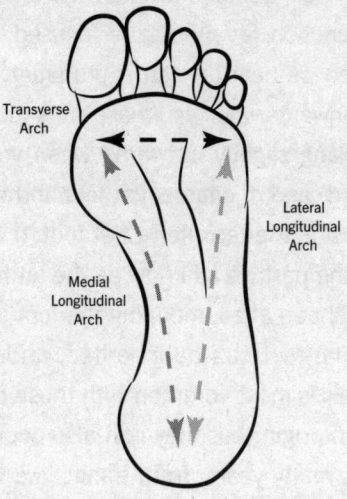

The foot is such an intricate part of our anatomy. It has twenty-six bones and over thirty ligaments. Many of the major muscles that we use in running, such as our calf muscles and tendons in the lower leg, are used and function because of the foot. It's why I place such value on it when it comes to running and injury. The foot's main role in the body is to aid us in locomotion (walking/running). In order to do that effectively, we must be able to absorb and spread the forces that occur when we take a step. The arches in our feet aid us in doing this. As you can see in the image above, the foot has three different arches: the medial, lateral and transverse.[1]

All of these arches, depending on how they function, will affect the overall ability of the foot to shock-absorb. This shock absorption is important to protect the bones, muscles and tendons throughout the lower limbs and spine.

The medial (longitudinal) arch is where most conversation around foot function for running is focused. This is the arch discussed when we hear the terms pronation (the natural way your foot rolls inwards when you make contact with the ground), supination (rolling slightly outwards when you make contact with the ground) and of course, flat feet and high arches.

'Pes Planus' is the term for a flat foot. It occurs when the longitudinal (the part we all know as the arch of the foot) has no dome-like shape at all, meaning the foot is fully contacted to the floor. Flat feet can be inherited, and from my clients I've noticed this is most common with those of a West-African or South-Asian origin; but they can also occur from daily life stressors over many years, from things like weight increases and poor footwear. Typical functions of flat feet are that they are poor shock absorbers, and people who have them tend to suffer from arch and ankle discomfort due to the limited support of the bone structure of that foot type.

On the opposite end of the scale, we have 'Pes Cavus', the high-arch foot. It's typically seen in those originating from the countries South Africa and Australia, which I've noted from my years of experience. Something intriguing about this foot type is that the longitudinal arch is high and so are the transverse and lateral arches. This creates a tripod of contact for the foot on the ground. This can increase the likelihood of shock absorption issues due to the rigidity of the foot structure, and has been found to increase the likelihood of lower limb overuse injuries.[2] Looking at both of these foot types, we can see they are at completely different ends of the spectrum and both can create increased likelihoods for discomfort and injury.

Now, I'm not saying this to scare you. Just because you have a high arch doesn't mean injury is coming for you, and if you have flat feet it doesn't mean that you shouldn't run. Having the knowledge of your own body and anatomy will help you to prevent these injuries and give you the power to understand the strength work you can do to better your foot function, no matter your arch shape. Strengthening, specifically foot-strengthening exercises, is the foundation of building full-body strength. In the foot, we have so many muscles and tendons, but the main muscle that runs through our medial arch is the tibialis posterior. It begins underneath the big toe joint and inserts within the calf belly. It aids with pronation of the foot and stabilization. This is the muscle we need to work on to help with not only strengthening the foot but aiding in its movement control.

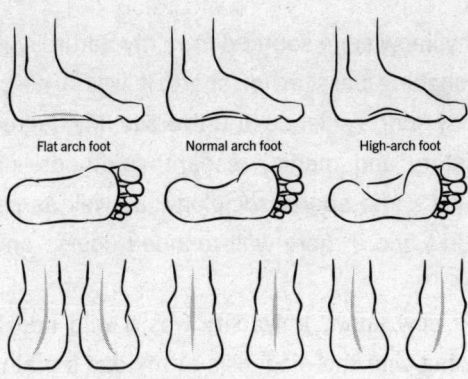

Flat arch foot   Normal arch foot   High-arch foot

Here are some strengthening exercises you can adopt a couple of times a week to aid in your foot strength:

- **Walking in barefoot shoes**

  This can help to strengthen your feet by allowing the small stabilizing muscles in them and your ankles to engage more actively.

- **Toe pianos**

  Toe pianos are a foot-strengthening exercise where you lift and lower each toe individually, like playing piano keys, to improve toe mobility, coordination and neuromuscular control.

- **Big-toe mobility**

  Adding in calf raises where you hold a tennis ball between your ankles before raising up your heels, can help with mobilizing the big toe. Limited big toe mobility can lead to compensations up the chain, which can lead to ankle, knee or hip issues.

With all my knowledge sourced from my Saturday job, alongside my ongoing passion for sport, it was a no-brainer for me to study sports science at university. My degree covered sports history and media, research methods, physiology, biomechanics and sports sociology, as well as psychology. You couldn't find a more well-rounded course on all things sport.

As you now know, university was a wild ride for me as I was dealing with the diagnosis of my dad's brain tumour. I had taken on so much, from athletics training to the netball team to my part-time job. The job was at a small, independent run shop, and it was a great escape. Here, I was able to further my passion for footwear and gait analysis, but I also had the pleasure of shadowing an insightful physio. As an ex-international 400m athlete, he understood how athletes move and train. He allowed me, in quiet times, to observe him and help in assessing the issues his clients were presenting. We would talk after client appointments to aid my understanding of the development of injury and also the treatment methods, through the use of correct footwear and exercises. Looking back, it was there that I realized how much power there was in having knowledge of your own body and how it works, for an injured athlete. I felt excited to learn further for my degree and arm myself with the tools to help and empower those in the running space, like you.

In my second year, I began working at Nike Town London in central London. This place was a hub for all things footwear and fashion, and it's where I made so many incredible friends. It was a place I felt welcomed and accepted due to the diverse group of people I had the pleasure of working with, and I'll forever have great memories of working with the team on the shop floor. Working in this shop taught me so much, especially about how to run. I was known as the girl who did the gait analysis. We had a treadmill on the shop floor for clients to test out shoes, and I was always there to help.

What Is Gait Analysis and Why You Need It

By performing a gait analysis, we can understand how a person moves when running or walking and assess their need for certain footwear, strength work and form improvements. This understanding is to help prevent your likelihood of injury and cater your shoes and strength work to help you succeed in running. Through this process, your gait cycle (this begins when one foot touches the ground, loads weight and then pushes off again before another stride repeats the process) can be analyzed. One phase of the cycle is when you spend time in contact with the ground, and the other is when you don't (when the foot is in the air). Gait and injury prevention research shows that mid-stance (the moment when you are on one leg and flexing your knee most in the gait cycle) is where the majority of injury occurs. It's why this phase of the gait cycle is where most of your running movement is analyzed during a gait analysis.

The Stride (Gait) Cycle

Many of your local running shops will have a gait service — always ask. It will likely involve stepping on a treadmill and running either barefoot or in your current shoes. They will then, based on your movements, gauge what footwear will be ideal for you. As you go through the footwear selection process, trying on different pairs of trainers, they will compare the shoes against each other on the treadmill and see which are functioning best for you and your body.

The shop I worked in that had the biggest impact on my career was Profeet. Founded in 2001, Profeet's goal is to bring the advantages experienced by top athletes to everyone. They bring together biomechanical knowledge, advanced analysis technologies, custom insoles and footwear expertise for the everyday runner and skier. I spent five years as part of this incredible team and owe a lot of my knowledge to them. My biggest learning was that every single runner is completely unique. A solution that works for one runner is not guaranteed to work for everyone with that exact same issue.

The Running Shoe

You now know your foot shape and function and how to strengthen it. You understand the process of how someone can analyze your running through a gait analysis and what the gait cycle for running is like, so let's look at the final piece of the puzzle when it comes to your feet and running: the shoes. Running footwear was and always will be my favourite thing to learn about. I love the idea that a shoe can help a person run in their most comfortable and most efficient state. The right shoes can help someone overcome injury and open up new possibilities of what a runner can achieve.

What excites me most, aside from the pretty colours (yes, I'm still swayed by this), is the constant evolution and growth of technology in this field. My very first running shoe was a Nike Pegasus 23 in 2006. I remember being so excited that my mum was buying them for me, my first proper pair of running trainers. I cherished them and wore them to death, until my foot came out the side of the shoe. I was so upset, and I cried when we threw them out. For me, that shoe represented my first-ever 'professional' shoe, like a badge of honour to say I was an athlete. Those shoes were the beginning of my sporting life.

As mentioned, every foot is different. Just like every footwear brand is different. One of the best books I read growing up was *Shoe Dog* by Phil Knight. It tells the story of the creation and birth of Blue Ribbon Sports, known as Nike today. I studied this book in detail, to understand the mindset needed to create a business, but alongside that mindset, the chaos and drama that building a business entails. Reading it really allowed me to understand footwear design, creation and the manufacturing process that occurs when creating a shoe.

The makeup of shoes since *Shoe Dog* was written has inherently remained the same. There are three key functions that as a runner it's important we know about footwear. Let's take a bottom-up approach, looking at the illustrations below:

Outsole: This is the sole of the shoe, the part that makes contact with the ground. Designers decide the surface/terrain the shoe is to be utilized for and that then dictates the elements used on the sole, such as different rubbers and lug types from the likes of Vibram or even a Michelin tyre.

Midsole: This is the component many will know as the cushioning part. This is where the level of support of a shoe is decided. Foam, known as EVA, is the most common component. It's a stretchy rubber-like polymer which is created by mixing ethylene and vinyl acetate.

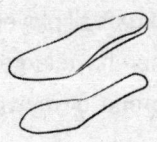

Carbon plate: This won't be in every shoe but is a component highlighted by many as a 'must' for runners. (It isn't by the way, and I'll explain why later.) It's a property that stiffens the shoe and, for runners, can increase the power and speed at which they propel off of the ground.

Upper: This part of the shoe is the one that makes contact with the top of the foot. This is actually where a vast amount of stability also comes from. You can have a support cushioning midsole, but if the upper isn't contacting your foot or holding you securely then the materials beneath it can't do their job.

Now you know the makeup of the shoe, let's discuss finding the correct type of shoe for you. This can be an absolute minefield for a lot of runners. There is so much information out there: from websites telling you the best deals, conflicting information on what is the latest best shoe for running from the big corporate brands, and your local running friends telling you what they run in and that it would be good for you. *What should you do?*

Gait analysis is your best friend. Through getting your gait analyzed, science can guide you to the answer of what shoes will work for you, rather than being swayed by anything else. There are some key things that can come up in an analysis. To start with, let us talk about shoe size. This can be a hang-up for some people, at least I struggled with having bigger feet growing up. It wasn't until I heard England netball players mention that the most successful sports women have larger-than-normal feet, like mine, that I became proud of my UK 8.5 feet.

With this in mind, let's talk about how big (or small) you need your trainers to be. For an ideal running shoe fit, you want to have the space of the width of your thumb between the end of your longest toe and the end of the shoe. If in doubt, when you are getting your gait analyzed the people in the store should be able to advise.

Next, I have to cover a word bandied about in the industry so much that many don't really understand its meaning or how to truly define it: pronation.

Pronation: Is It Bad?

Pronation is the rolling inwards of your feet. One of the biggest misconceptions is that pronation is bad. It's a natural movement that 99 per cent of feet do to help your body absorb the shock from the ground. Pronation, in some eyes, is deemed bad as when it's excessive it can begin to alter bodily mechanics further up, such as causing the knees to rotate inwards and the hips to shift side to side. Pronation has still not been proven to be a sole causer of injury.

A notable study from R. Nielsen et al in 2004 took almost 1000 runners and studied their running over a year.[3] The research was insightful and found that people who pronated were actually less likely to develop injury than those who didn't. There are so many other factors involved that a lot more research on general populations need to be carried out. Yet up until the past few years, the footwear industry had always sold shoes with the claim that the shoe will stop overpronation. Why am I telling you this? As you involve yourself more in the running space, you will hear people say that they want to stop their pronation and that if you have it, it's a problem for your running. I'm here to tell you that your pronation may not be 'bad'. Your pronation may be how your body likes to shock-absorb; what actually needs to be looked at is how that pronation interacts with your knees, hips and whole body. This will determine if it truly is bad for you, as a unique individual who runs.

Neutral/Supination: Is This Good?

Supination is simply outwards movement of the foot, causing more force to happen on the lateral side of the foot. The type of foot that makes this movement is usually more rigid and will use the lateral (outer) part of the foot to shift weight to. It's rare and only a small percentage of the population have supinated feet.

With footwear, we're not concerned with the angle of the foot in a standing position or how the arches look in that position either. Arch height is also not a predeterminant for the level of support one needs. A high arch doesn't necessarily mean the foot is neutral and won't pronate, neither does a low arch or flat foot definitely mean a foot will pronate badly. The opposite can be true of both. It's so specific person to person that we can't make assumptions of how a foot will move based on its shape/structure. We care about the movement through the running stride and how the ankle joint moves in relation to the knee and hip joints during that stride pattern.

Having discussed the main types of movement of the foot, it makes sense to discuss how footwear has a part to play in relation to the movement of the foot. A foot that pronates excessively and causes an increased stress on the knees medially will usually benefit from a more supportive shoe.

Support Shoes

A support shoe is a type of shoe that tries to stop and control excessive pronation. It's traditionally made up of two densities of foam. One is softer to help shock-absorb at initial contact, and one is a firmer, more dense foam (also known as a shoe post) to help control the area in which the foot pronates. This can be in the rear of the foot on the inside of the arch or in the middle of the foot, depending on how much support the shoe model is offering. The highest level of support shoe is the one with dense rear-foot support. Every foot can pronate to a differing degree, hence why there are multiple types of support shoes.

Neutral Shoes

Neutral shoes are a type of shoe with the sole purpose of guiding the runner from initial contact with the ground to pushing off it. They are simpler and traditionally have one or multiple densities of foam throughout the entire sole. Some of these foams can be soft; some can be firmer and more responsive. There are also some neutral shoes that have layers of differing foam densities. None of these models have any support in them.

Carbon-Plate Shoes

Have you heard about or seen carbon-plate running shoes? They're notably worn by some of the fastest runners in the world and take centre stage when it comes to world marathon events. Carbon shoes, also known as 'super shoes', have carbon plates throughout the soles. Research has shown that this shoe type does have great benefits to improve your running economy compared to other types of footwear.[4] Brands combine these stiff, powerfully responsive plates with foam to create a light and fast shoe. This shoe has come to be popular with many runners but should be used with caution.

As a new runner, you don't need this shoe. Focus on comfort. If you are considering a carbon shoe, look to use it sporadically in your training and even save it for race days. Constant use of carbon shoes has been shown to reduce muscular use over time and can increase injury risk in the foot too.[5] Yes, carbon shoes can make you more efficient and run faster but I'd utilize them as a tool, rather than the only shoe you would use to run in.

Overall, footwear is so individual to the runner. There may be a shoe your new running friend swears by and says it's comfy and supportive. You may try on the exact same shoe in a running shop and it doesn't work for you, leaving you feeling like you are running through sand. Footwear can look at support or softness, different shapes of shoe for different foot shapes and widths, there is such variety. One task I loved when at Profeet was sitting down as a team and deciding where the new footwear for that season would sit, ranging from most to least supportive. As I transitioned to manager and beyond, I continued this constant learning. It's another reason I love footwear so much, every year there are constant changes by brands, from technological advances and popularity of events in the running world.

Drop Height of Footwear

Drop height is the difference between the height of cushioning in the heel and the height in the forefoot. For example, a shoe with a drop of 4mm may have 24mm of cushioning in the heel and 20mm in the forefoot. The higher the drop of the shoe, the less stress on the calf muscles to work as hard. If you have any history of calf issues or Achilles problems, be cautious in your shoe choice when it comes to drop height.

One of the joys of working for Profeet was what is known to those in the footwear industry as 'sell-ins'. This is a period where all the brands either invite you to their offices or they come to your shop, to show you the shoes for the coming seasons. I was a Running Buyer for four years at Profeet, with the final two years focusing solely on footwear. It was a role I adored. My geeky brain loves numbers and analyzing sales and percentages of what worked with our clients, and projecting figures for further seasons was a role I thrived in.

For the 'sell-in' of autumn/winter 2017, Saucony, one of the highest-performing brands, brought us their trail shoe for an elevated session. We took the shoe down to the Thames Path and took it for a swift run. I was panting like an old dog while my fellow colleagues floated like gazelles. Ten kilometres later, my calves felt a bit tight but I thought nothing of it. The next morning though, every muscle fibre in my calves was on fire. Why? The new model of the shoe was the Saucony Peregrine, a light, responsive trail shoe with an only 4mm drop. Up until this point, I had only ever run in 8- or 10mm-drop shoes. My calves were shocked that day and for the following three days after. The muscles were weak, but I'd also introduced something brand new to the mix and assumed I could just run the same distance as I had before. I learned a lesson that day.

This is not to say you can't use low-drop shoes but maybe consider easing yourself in to them (unlike me) or only using them for shorter distances. Does a lower drop height increase the likelihood of injury? In 2016, researchers from Luxembourg Institute for Health carried out a study with over 500 runners running over a six-month period in a range of shoes. Some were 0mm drop (barefoot style), some were 6mm and the last were 10mm. Across all the runners, only 25 per cent of them became injured. Out of those 25 per cent, there was little to no difference across all three types of shoe. Further research has suggested that a drop of 7–10mm helps to provide better shock absorption and protect the foot and ankle.[6] As a rule personally, I lean towards that drop for all of my footwear.

Barefoot Running — Is It Really the Answer?

It's hard to talk about footwear without giving an insight on barefoot shoes. You may have heard of these before. The idea behind these shoes was born from the knowledge that our ancestors that roamed the savannas of Africa were running barefoot. They had strong feet and were able to be strong and chase down prey and walk around all day.

The barefoot concept isn't new at all, but the conversation was reignited after the publishing of the book *Born to Run* by Christopher McDougall. The book details our history and origins as humans and documents the immense journey of Chris. It discusses his experiences on his journey to reduce his ongoing injuries by seeing the ways of the Tarahumara people. As the book progresses, Christopher interviews Dr Daniel Lieberman. Lieberman is an anthropologist at Harvard, dealing in all things to do with the historical origins of humans and, in this case, how they moved. In the book, he makes a very convincing argument for the natural, more minimal, barefoot style of running. He states, 'many running injuries are caused by our feet being weak . . . Before Nike in 1972, people ran in thin-soled shoes and had a much lower incidence of knee injuries.'

Born to Run shares with us that, by adding a shoe to the foot, we reduce the body's use of our natural movement and therefore encourage runners to use their heels to strike the ground. The heel strike causes more impact in the legs, which calls for additional running-shoe cushioning, according to the book. Ultimately, his argument is that running shoes created by the big mover at the time, Nike, caused injuries and so the brand fed its own demand.

I hear this way of thinking and agree that we have altered the shapes and mechanics of feet by putting them into shoes. As a sports scientist and someone who has analyzed thousands of feet, I agree that this method of running barefoot may work for some and there can be many positives. Using shoes like Vivos and Altras not only give the foot more space to move naturally from a width perspective but also increases the likelihood of mid–fore foot striking, which is seen as one of the most efficient ways to run. It *must* be noted, however, that reverting to wearing barefoot shoes takes a lot of time and patience that many runners don't have. Many I know who transferred started over a six-month period to rebuild muscles in their feet by first walking in barefoot shoes, before slowly building 1km at a time to allow the body to adapt. It can be done but, like anything, isn't suitable for all. I've witnessed runners who will only ever run barefoot and those who no matter how hard they try, their natural biomechanics don't allow for it.

As I keep coming back to, what shoe works best for you is entirely subjective. If you consistently run in footwear that doesn't align with your body mechanics it can increase your likelihood of injury. Imagine a foot that supinates (all the force landing on the outside of the foot) going into a support shoe (a shoe that forces them to the outside of the foot even more). That support shoe will further increase their angle of foot supination. This negative alteration of mechanics at foot level will lead to increased lateral stress on the knees and become a one-way ticket to ITB (iliotibial band) irritation and other potential injury risks. The same is true for the softness of footwear. If a shoe is too soft for a runner, the runner may struggle to propel off the ground. This can throw all sorts of injuries into the mix, so remember: a personalized approach when selecting running shoes is key.[7]

Lacing

Once you have the right shoe that feels comfortable and fits your foot shape and mechanics, lacing may be something to consider to help customize your fit further. For more information on this, I've gathered some different key techniques, which you can watch here:

I hope that in this chapter you've learned that there is no one like you. Your body mechanics and foot shape and function are completely unique. From foot width to arch height to foot size, it's impossible for me to answer that age old question: what is the best running shoe? What I can say is that, out there, there will be a running shoe that is best for *you*. The many years and experiences through my education have taught me so much. I still perform one-to-one analysis on runners and even now can say I've never seen the same feet or mechanics twice. Every one of us is magically individual. I hope you can now make a more informed decision, knowing that the tech, the science and the potential for what could help you is the biggest key to unlocking your running potential.

KEY TAKEAWAYS:

- All feet are different. Different foot shapes mean different types of functionality.

- Pronation is not bad but is how the foot shock-absorbs. It's the degree and speed of pronation which can become problematic for injury issues.

- Shoe brands serve different foot shapes. A brand may be better for you only because the shape of the shoe is a better fit than another, not because they are the 'best' brand for shoes.

- Gait analysis will help you find the shoe for you.

- You don't need the latest and most expensive shoe to run, you need the right shoe for your foot shape and function.

- Barefoot shoes aren't for everyone, in the same way that carbon shoes aren't for everyone. The can both be used as a tool for further improvements in running.

- Knowledge is power.

FINDING SPEED

In the running world, speed is such a layered conversation. Some people define themselves by the pace they can run at. For those at the elite level, seconds can be the difference between Olympic Gold and fourth place, the difference between being a 'success' and a 'failure'. That is the ruthlessness of professional sport. For you and I, who aren't elite runners, this doesn't have to apply. Although social media may have you think that holding a 7- or 8-minute km isn't impressive, I'm here to tell you it is. Running full stop is impressive. Saying this, as you move through your running journey, you may wish to improve your speed for certain distances or you may simply be intrigued to see what your body can do.

I must also share that getting faster really isn't a necessity. You think at eighty, I'll still be running the same paces I am at thirty? It would be a miracle but very unlikely. Does that mean I won't have the passion to run? Of course not! I plan to run throughout my life. Some seasons, I'll look to continually get faster. Some I won't. Please know, being able to run freely without time or pace as a factor is a valid and wonderful place to stay.

When running the Chicago Marathon last year, I'll never forget seeing a sign that said: 'forwards is a pace'. I think that message fits here. I don't wish this chapter to make you feel pressured into trying to constantly improve, however, if you have the urge to see where you can go with it, then this section is for you. We are going to explore how to run at different paces, look at different workouts to help your running and explore what pace and effort progression looks like. With improving your running, strength plays a huge part. As you know, I've had some severe injuries in the past. Without strength training, I wouldn't have recovered from my inability to walk without pain, I wouldn't still be running, and running my fastest races, all these years later. Let me help you find running easier, by improving your running economy.

Benchmarks

Whether it's a 5k run, 10k or further, having a timed, maximal effort (running as fast as you can) is a great starting point to build from, because it gives you a benchmark of where your pace is at. This could be completed on a parkrun on a Saturday, where you can receive a free timed 5k effort, or in your own time as a time trial on any given day where you feel good enough to run your fastest for the distance.

Start Getting Faster

Once you have your benchmark of how fast you can run at maximum effort for the distance, it's time for the challenge of getting faster. First, we need to address that running doesn't always have to be carried out at the same speed. Variety is the spice of life and the same applies with your running. The more variety in your pace, the better your body can recover and also conquer the overall goal of getting faster.

When beginning to understand different types of runs, it's important to understand RPE as one type of measure, aside from simple paces in both miles and kilometres. **RPE** stands for 'rate of perceived exertion' and is measured on a scale of one to ten. One is an easy walk on a Sunday morning with a coffee and baked good in hand (I'd go for a cinnamon roll), and ten is maximal, all-out effort that has you completely out of breath. When addressing an improvement in your speed, we can create a plan with both easy and faster-paced runs in your week to gain the greatest effective outcome.

Easy runs are as described: easy. It's a pace that is conversational that you can keep holding for a long period of time. **Recovery runs** also fall into this category. These would register a 2–3 on the scale of RPE.

Speed runs are runs which incorporate very hard sustained efforts with rest or can be non-stop sustained efforts, also known as **Tempo runs** (and sometimes called **Threshold runs**). Some speed runs may involve intervals and times when you are required to rest and walk to recover. Most speed-based runs register anywhere from a 5–9 effort level when in the working zone (the running interval of a workout).

Another common metric used in running is **heart rate (HR)**. Heart rate monitors give live and direct real-time data for the amount of times your heart is being per minute (BPM). Every person's HR is different and many factors affect the numbers, from age to fitness level and underlying health conditions. As a simple rule, there are five zones, with Zone 1 the lowest intensity and Zone 5 the maximum full-on, out-of-breath effort you could give.

With your new benchmark time, you can include speed runs alongside other easy-paced runs to enhance your speed. That is how you can decrease your benchmark time. Interval training is one of the best exercises for physiological adaptation to running.[1] Studies have found it enhances the endurance of runners by improving maximal oxygen uptake, running economy and muscular adaptations. To put it more simply, interval training increases your ability to run longer because your body is able to adapt to utilizing more oxygen. This extra oxygen aids in helping the muscles to work harder, more powerfully, and therefore helps you to run more efficiently. What does being efficient mean when it comes to running? Think back to our discussion of running economy (on page 147). It means that more of the energy your muscles are creating is going directly into propelling you forwards.

Speed Sessions — the What, the How and the Why

Below are three key speed sessions you can use and progress to improve your running economy and therefore, your 5km time. These can be timed on a phone, a watch or on a treadmill, and I'd advise keeping a note in your phone or using a notebook to write down your intervals and time taken for them. This way you can know your progress and be proud of your work. These speed runs would be added once a week as your hard run. For example, if you run three times a week, keep two runs easy still (RPE 3) then have one speed run (RPE 8+). With all of the intervals below, rest time is meant to help you recover and bring your heart rate down. Walking is the best way to aid with this recovery as it keeps the blood and oxygen pumping to the muscles so they can replenish to run again. As you advance in your running, you may find you can recover in a light jog; I wouldn't advise this unless you have performed these intervals all the way through first.

8–14 REPS

	NUMBER OF INTERVALS	DISTANCE OF INTERVAL	REST AFTER INTERVAL
Week 1	6	400m	2 min
Week 2	8	400m	2 min
Week 3	10	400m	2 min
Week 4	12	400m	2 min

	NUMBER OF INTERVALS	DISTANCE OF INTERVAL	REST AFTER INTERVAL
Week 5	8	400m	1 min 45 sec
Week 6	10	400m	1 min 45 sec
Week 7	12	400m	1 min 45 sec
Week 8	14	400m	1 min 45 sec
Week 9	8	400m	1 min 30 sec
Week 10	10	400m	1 min 30 sec

This workout is a physical and mental challenge. 400-metre intervals are special because doing them repeatedly not only forces the heart to work harder but also builds a strong mindset. Performing intervals at a high intensity with short rest periods helps to improve our body's ability to utilize oxygen, especially when reps are high in both quantity and quality. The goal of a 400m interval workout is to hit the same time for each interval performed – this is a one-way ticket to progressive improvement. All running leads to physical progress but with this workout, the mental fortitude is unmatched, too. Check out the table, which breaks down how you could look to progress each effort weekly.

Repeating 400m reps eight to twelve times, with rest gradually reducing from two minutes down to one minute and thirty seconds over the weeks, is character-building! In some marathon training blocks, I've taken this session up to twenty reps with a one-minute rest between intervals. With this workout, the key is to try to stay consistent with your pace for each repetition. For example, if intervals 1, 2 and 3 are 2:15, but intervals 5 and 6 drift to 2:30, your feedback for your next session next would be to start the first few intervals slightly slower.

There are workouts that I still go out too fast on and then hang on for dear life in the closing runs. Every day is a school day, no matter how long you've been running.

5 X 1KM

The humbling 1km interval is designed to build your speed endurance. The goal with these intervals is to hold them at a RPE 8, a pace I like to also call 'comfortably uncomfortable'. One that you would love to take a rest from but know you can, with some mental battles, hold for the distance. Rest will remain the same for the first four weeks, then reduce gradually over the following weeks to three minutes, progressively dropping down to as little as two minutes or less. This is to elicit a challenging effort which the body has to adapt and recover from quickly. Rest here is a walk or *very* light jog. Over time, you will begin to see a time frame pattern of what your 1km time is. The goal? To keep this as consistent as possible.

	NUMBER OF INTERVALS	DISTANCE OF INTERVAL	REST AFTER EACH INTERVAL
Week 1	5	1km	3 min
Week 2	6	1km	3 min
Week 3	7	1km	3 min
Week 4	8	1km	3 min
Week 5	5	1km	2 min 30 sec

	NUMBER OF INTERVALS	DISTANCE OF INTERVAL	REST AFTER EACH INTERVAL
Week 6	6	1km	2 min 30 sec
Week 7	7	1km	2 min 30 sec
Week 8	8	1km	2 min 30 sec
Week 9	5	1km	2 min
Week 10	6	1km	2 min

On workouts with 1km intervals, I like to split my reps in half mentally. This way I can then count down on my reps once I pass halfway. For example, in a 6 x 1km session, I'll only think about the first 3 reps. Once I hit halfway, I can then count down the efforts remaining and mentally I feel like I'm more capable.

400M/600M/800M/1KM/800M/600M/400M

This is known as a pyramid session and is one I use to aid runners in understanding how to hold back their pace. Pyramids are sessions where the runs gradually increase in length and then decrease back down. They're programmed firstly to add variety to training, to keep you guessing and feeling out each run length as you work through the workout. Physiologically, the different distances help you find where the point of discomfort lies. Are you ready to tackle your mile pace for 800m or maybe further? Where is your sticky distance point? This workout will be that sweet-spot test.

You will work your way up the ladder, holding paces faster

than your 5km pace for the 400m and 600m intervals, resting 90 seconds after each interval. Then, for the 800m and 1km intervals you will hit your goal 5km pace with 2 minutes and 2.5 minutes rest respectively after. For this session, we have a change from the previous workouts, in that after two weeks the suggested progression is definitively jogging your recovery. Jogging your recovery will actually help flush out the lactic acid you build up during the working interval faster than walking, it will increase the amount of oxygen resupplied to the muscles and after your workout you'll recover quicker. I've placed the jog only in the third and fourth week, as it can be more mentally challenging than anything. Aim for the pace to be a 2–3 RPE for the recovery jog effort.

DISTANCE OF INTERVAL	WEEK 1 REST AFTER INTERVAL	WEEK 2 REST AFTER INTERVAL	WEEK 3 REST AFTER INTERVAL	WEEK 4 REST AFTER INTERVAL
400m	200m walk/jog	200m walk/jog	200m jog	200m jog
600m	300m walk/jog	300m walk/jog	300m jog	300m jog
800m	400m walk/jog	400m walk/jog	400m jog	400m jog
1km	500m walk/jog	500m walk/jog	500m jog	500m jog
800m	400m walk/jog	400m walk/jog	400m jog	400m jog
600m	300m walk/jog	300m walk/jog	300m jog	300m jog
400m	200m walk/jog	200m walk/jog	200m jog	200m jog

Rest Is the Best Tool to Improve

Rest is essential, both generally and when you are looking to improve your speed. Whether as part of your training plan or just generally in day-to-day training, including some lower-intensity runs and increased rest will allow your body to regulate and to adapt to the stress and demands you have placed it under. A deload is something that all runners should incorporate into their plan. It's a period in your training where intensity and load is reduced to allow the body to recover. This can be a 20–30 per cent decrease in mileage or can look like less intensity across your miles, as well as extra rest elements in your week. For many with life and external commitments, it may happen naturally. Some weeks you can't train with the intensity you wish because life gets in the way and sessions are missed. This is totally okay, no matter what your running ability is. Your most intense training can be structured around when your body is working in your favour. There are pros and cons to this, but here is one option:

Some people work better on six- or even eight-week cycles where they progressively build (increase the volume of miles run) over that time and have a deload week. For example, if I'm marathon training, a twenty-week cycle could look like four weeks of increasing your mileage and strength intensity, then a one-week deload. The table below shows twenty weeks of cycle. In four week blocks, you can see the progression. You will then be running your peak mileage three weeks out from the race and then taper progressively into race day.

Tapering is the art of reducing the volume of your training (in mileage and length of time) to allow the body to recover and be in the most rested state come race day.

Week 1	New week	Week 6	New week	Week 11	New week	Week 16	Build
Week 2	Build	Week 7	Build	Week 12	Build	Week 17	Peak
Week 3	Build	Week 8	Build	Week 13	Build	Week 18	Deload/ Taper
Week 4	Peak	Week 9	Peak	Week 14	Peak	Week 19	Deload/ Taper
Week 5	Deload	Week 10	Deload	Week 15	Deload	Week 20	Taper/ Race

For those with a menstrual cycle, you could consider adapting your deload week to when your PMS is at its strongest. This will allow a reduction in higher-intensity efforts when, potentially, energy levels may be lower.

Easy = Easy, so Hard = Hard

A second major change you can make to your training is the simple premise of making your easy runs easy and your hard runs hard. From the years of HIIT (High Intensity Interval Training) being a buzzword in the fitness space, many runners are too focused on running hard all the time. We don't always have to give RPE 9/10. Let's show ourselves some love. Running easy will help with building your speed endurance.

At a scientific level, this means at a pace where you're at less than 70 per cent of your maximal heart rate. This zone is also known as Zone 2.

We do this in order to build our mitochondrial density. Mitochondria are the breathing powerhouses of our cells. The more mitochondria we have, the stronger our aerobic (breathing with oxygen) system is, ultimately improving our bodies' ability to run for longer.[2] What makes this even more magic is that having *more* mitochondria also helps with the breakdown of the waste products that slow our body down when we run fast. You likely will have experienced lactic acid, the feeling of legs burning like fire and then, as you muster the will to push through it, a heavy sluggish feeling that radiates through what feels like your mind, body and soul. Want to get rid of that? Combine a few easy runs with a speed run in your week and, over time, the adaptations will occur to enable your body to hold faster paces for longer.

Find Zone 2 Impossible While Running?

To run well, you need your body's ability to process and utilize oxygen to be high. Especially as a new runner, your heart rate may skyrocket when running, and the thought of it being low or feeling like a 3/4 RPE may seem way off into the future. What you can do to still achieve all the benefits of Zone 2 training is to take the exercise on in a different form – maybe cycling, hiking or even swimming. Zone 2 work can be improved through any exercise. Maybe you can involve your families on weekend hikes, you can cycle, use the cross trainer or even swim. Our hearts understand the demands we require of them to beat faster. Exercising in multiple forms and modalities aside from just running, will actually keep you more interested in your training and even have you more excited to run by doing it less.

I spoke to Janie Perry, who is a registered nutritional therapist practitioner, to talk about the importance of nutrition and running. If you're looking to improve your speed or gain strength (more on this soon) what you eat is important. Here are some of her top tips on fuelling to get the best out of your running:

Fuelling for Running and Strength: A Simple Guide

1. Running
Fuelling correctly is key to optimal performance, helping you feel good during and after your run, together with boosting your recovery. The length of time and intensity of each session will dictate when and how best to fuel. As a keen marathon runner myself, I know how easy it is to get fuelling wrong but also how easy it is to get it right and what a difference it makes.

Fuelling for a run of less than 30 minutes

Before:
There is normally no need to fuel before a 30-minute run. Your body's preferred source of energy is carbohydrates, and you have enough stored in the body in the form of glycogen to last 60–90 minutes.

During:
No additional fuel is needed for this short duration.

After:
Refuel as soon as possible to boost recovery, focusing on carbo-hydrates to replenish glycogen stores and protein to help repair and rebuild muscle. Good choices include chocolate milk, a protein shake with clean protein powder, berries or peanut butter on toast (sourdough, rye or wholegrain). If you choose to use protein powders, always look for ones with no artificial flavourings, sweeteners or colours.

There is no need to hydrate unless you have been running in extreme heat.

If you want an extra boost to help your recovery, you could include foods containing omega-3 fatty acids, healthy fats, in your post-exercise snack or at the very least at the next main meal, to help reduce inflammation. Good choices include chia seeds, flaxseed (both good to add into smoothies), walnuts and oily fish (for example, salmon, mackerel, anchovies, sardines and herring).

Fuelling for a run of 30–60 minutes

Before:
Fuelling here depends on when your last meal was and the type of session ahead.
- Easy run: Fuelling is not absolutely necessary.
- Intense run: If the planned session is hard or you haven't eaten for a while, consume 20–30g of carbohydrates before heading out. Good choices include a medium-sized banana, apple purée pouch, energy gel or energy drink, or half a bagel with jam or peanut butter.

During:

There is no need to fuel unless the run is high intensity. If so, 20–30g of carbohydrates in the form of a gel or a carbohydrate sports drink. This depends on whether it's hot and/or if you tend to sweat a lot. Carry water with electrolytes if appropriate.

After:

The advice here is the same as the 'Fuelling for a run of less than 30 minutes' category – refuel with carbohydrates and protein. Add in foods containing omega-3 fatty acids (as above) where you can.

Fuelling for a run of 60 minutes to 4 hours

If it's practicable to get up 3–4 hours before you start, have a meal consisting of complex carbohydrates and some protein. Good choices include: a bagel with jam or peanut butter, oats with protein powder, scrambled eggs on toast or yogurt with some banana or honey. Keep fibre to a minimum, so opt for white bread and avoid nuts and seeds to avoid any gut distress later in your run. The aim is to finish eating 3 hours before your start time, to give the body time to fully digest the meal. Just before you start your run, have a banana, apple purée pouch, gel or carb drink.

If a meal 3–4 hours before you start your run isn't practicable, make sure you have eaten well the day before so that your glycogen stores are topped up, and have a banana, apple purée pouch, gel or carb drink just before you start.

During:
- Fuel every 20–30 minutes. Aim for at least 30–60g of carbo-hydrates per hour. The more intense the session, the more the carbohydrate requirement.
- Use sports gels, energy drinks, chews or real food. It's a personal choice and about what works for you. Real food like bagels, fruit (fresh or dried), honey, homemade energy balls or salted potatoes is an attractive option but may be difficult to carry and eat if you are racing.
- Set an alert on your watch for every 20–30 minutes to fuel consistently.
- Hydration: Drink water with electrolytes to avoid hypo-natraemia (low sodium levels). As a general guide, aim for 475–700ml per hour.

After:
Refuel immediately with carbohydrates and protein. See 'Fuelling for a run of less than 30 minutes' for good choices.

Include omega-3s (salmon, chia seeds, flaxseeds) to reduce inflammation immediately after your run or at your next meal. See 'Fuelling for a run of less than 30 minutes' for food examples.

Hydrate with water for the rest of the day. If the weather has been hot and you have a high sweat rate, you may want to add some electrolytes. A sign that you are well hydrated is when your urine is clear or a pale yellow.

Fuelling for a run of 6+ hours

Before:
- Eat a full meal 3–4 hours before, containing complex carbo-hydrates and protein. See 'Fuelling for a run of 60 minutes to 4 hours' for more details.

- Before you start running, consume 20–30g of carbohydrates (gel, energy bar, carbohydrate drink or real food like a medium-sized banana or half a white bagel).

During:
- Fuel every 20–30 minutes, aiming for 60–90g of carbohydrates per hour.
- Set an alert on your watch for every 20–30 minutes to fuel consistently.
- Runs of this distance require real food (savoury and sweet) as well as the fuels discussed above. Good options include salted potatoes, crisps, wraps filled with hummus, avocado, halloumi or tofu, cake, cheese sandwiches, bacon or pork pies.
- Liquid foods are a helpful addition as you are likely to experience a time when you don't feel like eating but continuing to take fuel on board is essential. Try flat coke, soups or electrolyte drinks. Coffee and tea are useful to add a caffeine boost to help with fatigue, focus and perceived rates of pain.
- Hydration: Drink water with electrolytes throughout, to avoid hyponatraemia (low sodium levels). As a general guide, aim for 475–700ml per hour but adjust amounts based on conditions and your own personal sweat rate.

After:
Refuel immediately with carbohydrates and protein. See 'Fuelling for a run of less than 30 minutes' for good choices.

Include omega-3 foods immediately after your run or at your next meal. See 'Fuelling for a run of less than 30 minutes' for food examples.

Hydrate with water for the rest of the day. See 'Fuelling for a run of 60 minutes to 4 hours' for more details.

General note:
If you are training for an event, make sure you practice your fuelling strategy before race day so that you know that it works for you. Don't try anything new on race day!

2. Strength work

Strength training is a game-changer for runners looking to improve performance and avoid injury. To get the most out of each session, protein is the key macronutrient.

For athletes, my general rule is 1.6–2g of protein per kg of body weight. So, for a 60kg athlete, that's 96–120g of protein, ideally, spaced throughout the day in three meals and two snacks.

If you've had a balanced meal including 20–40g of protein (depending on body weight) several hours before a strength session, there is no need to top up with a protein shake before you head to the gym. I always suggest an intake of 20–40g of protein within an hour after a training session to prevent muscle breakdown and help with repair.

Good examples of approximately 20g of protein include:

- 1 chicken or turkey breast
- 1 beef steak (grass-fed)
- 200g cottage cheese
- 1 piece of salmon
- 225g Greek or soya yogurt
- 1 pint of milk
- 3 eggs
- 1 average serving of protein powder (no added sugar, flavours or preservatives)
- 6 tablespoons of peanut butter

- 4 thin slices of halloumi
- 2 tablespoons of hemp seeds

Fuelling your body well is one of the most impactful things you can do to support your performance, recovery and overall wellbeing. As you can see, it's not just about eating more; it's about eating with purpose. By learning to time your intake, choose nutrient-rich foods and listen to your body's needs, you're laying the foundation for consistent energy, faster recovery and long-term progress. It might not go right the first time you try and your body may let you know what does and doesn't work but, the more you honour your body with the correct fuel, the more it will show up for you on those runs.

In my day to day, I always lean in to the Japanese idea of *kaizen*. Kaizen means continuous improvement. In other fields, you may hear it as the 1 per cent better every day idea. By adopting this mantra to my running, I'm able to make the smallest changes to ensure I'm improving continually. Whether that is taking more rest or performing that extra stretch routine, or whether that's nailing my speed session once a week as a minimum, I'll carry out the smallest steps to make a big improvement. That is how I wish you to improve too. When we decide to add or change multiple things, the overwhelming pressure that can bring can become a negative rather than positive. So, with all of the information you've taken from this chapter on improving your speed, I hope there are small changes you can put into your weekly training to come out faster, stronger and more confident in your running.

KEY TAKEAWAYS:

- Speed is relative. We all have our own running pace and wherever you are is valid.
- Interval training is a way to increase your speed and run for longer distances.
- Adding in one speed session a week is enough.
- Keep your easy runs easy and your hard ones hard. Know the difference.
- Zone 2 work is great for not only your running, but overall cardiovascular health.
- What you eat before, during and after runs matters. Food is your friend.

FINDING STRENGTH

When it comes to running, no matter who you are, strength is key. It's the foundation for you to not only be injury-free but also to improve your chances of longevity in running, and life. My first running injury was shin splints, and I thought it defined me as a runner at the time — that I was a failed runner because I'd got injured. What I now know is that it was part of my journey. I had to listen and understand what my body was able to manage in terms of mileage and load. Since then, I prevent reoccurrence with specific strength exercises. I monitor my mileage and have made changes to my overall training to ensure they never become an issue again.

As much as I want injury to be something you've heard about in mythical tales about running — and never experience yourself — there is a likelihood it may happen as you learn more about your body and its limits. I'd love you to be on this journey of running towards your next goal or distance or even just beginning to run, without being repeatedly stopped in your tracks by an injury. Some of you may be reading this having suffered an injury that is holding you back now or prevented you from getting back into running. I've collated a set of exercises to help with your journey to aid in the healing and prevention of further injury.

I'm not a physio or a medical professional, here to officially help you diagnose problems. I'm a gait specialist who has dealt with and helped thousands of runners overcome their injuries. If you have a running injury, please seek medical advice to come up with a specific diagnosis. My goal by the end of this chapter is for you to be armed with the tools to help armour your body so that injury can be a distant memory for you. This will also give you a strength routine in your toolbox, that you can use to become stronger than ever. I've included QR codes in this chapter that you can scan with your phone camera. These will link you to videos of strength-building exercises, so you can really visualize how to perform them correctly.

Shin Splints

WHAT ARE THEY?

Shin splints is the global term for any pain on the shin. Your shin is on the front of your lower leg and is made up of two bones, your fibula and tibia. The main muscle through the front of your shin is your tibialis anterior, and the muscle that runs medially and under the foot (inside leg) is the tibialis posterior. When pain occurs on the shin, it can present in many ways. There can be a singular sharp point of pain on the shin bone or there can be a dull ache through the inner shin (just up from your ankle bone). If you have any pain in the shin region, I advise you to seek professional medical advice.

HOW DOES IT HAPPEN?

Pain in the shin region can have several causes, but there are a few reasons you may get this pain from running. Overtraining and excessive loading of the lower leg can cause these issues. Without rest, massage or stretching, the repetitive nature of running can increase the stress on the calf and shin area causing discomfort. In addition, form issues, such as over-stride and low cadence can also increase the loading of forces through the lower leg.

WHAT EXERCISES CAN HELP IT?

With many of these injuries, my first guidance is always to rest. Taking running off the table, as hard as it may be, is the first step in helping your body recover. Once you are walking pain-free, I'd advise you then start with your lower leg strength rebuild.

The first strength exercise is the Tibialis Anterior Raise. Leaning with your back against a wall, walk your feet out about half a metre from the wall. Keeping your legs straight, raise your feet off the ground while keeping your heels down on the ground. This engages the shin muscles and will help increase lower leg strength.

Start with 3 sets of 10–12 reps, then increase the reps weekly until you reach 20 per set.

For the next exercise, we look at strengthening the gastro-cnemius with eccentric calf raises. The gastrocnemius, along with the soleus, is one of the two major muscles at the back of the lower leg. Find yourself a step, or if you don't have one, a sturdy book, and stand near a wall for balance. Standing on the edge of the step, rise onto the tips of your toes, and then, for a count of five, slowly lower your heels over the step as far as possible. Once lowered, rise onto your toes for a count of one. Repeat and build over time to 2–3 sets of 15–30 reps, resting for 60–90 seconds between sets. To progress, perform the exercise on one leg or add weight (such as dumbbells or tin cans) in each hand, doing 15–30 reps on each side.

Now for stretches – using the same step, drop your heel off it and actively push into your heel. With your leg straight, this will stretch the top portion of your calf and with a bent knee, it will stretch the lower portion. Hold for 20–30 seconds on each side. If this stretch sends pain to the front of your ankle, foam rolling is likely a better option for you.

Knee Pain

WHAT IS IT?

Knee pain can be any level of discomfort around the knee joint. Runner's knee (patellofemoral pain) and ITBS (iliotibial band syndrome) are two of the most common injuries which I came across in my time as a gait analyst.

HOW DOES IT HAPPEN?

The issue of runner's knee is mainly from overuse. Similarly to shin pain, quick increases in training volume or poor running form mechanics can inadvertently load the knee. This gives the feeling of a deep ache, which may turn into sharpness. Pain usually presents itself at the front of your kneecap.

ITB issues usually occur from similar overuse/overload, plus can be linked to an unstable pelvis and tension/weakness through the quad and hips. The main area of pain with ITBs is that outer knee (lateral), and it has a tendency to be sharp.

WHAT EXERCISES CAN HELP?

An exercise you can add in to benefit your knees is the split squat. Working this single-leg movement will not only strengthen your quadricep but also your glutes. It will encourage balance at foot level but also stability through the knee joint. It will also require you to develop the strength to not cry through the burn it delivers — you're welcome.

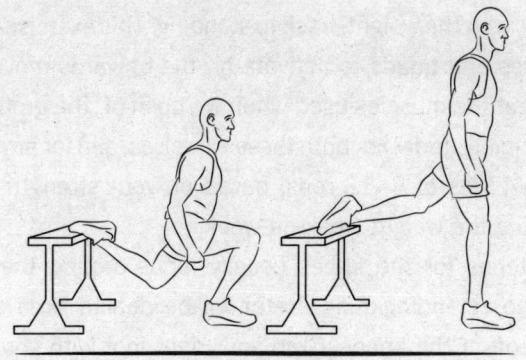

Start with your feet hip-width apart and parallel, like you're on a set of train tracks. As a main starting point for the length of your stride, start by placing the feet in a position that leaves the knees at about a 90-degree angle.

As you descend, the goal is to bend both knees at the same time while keeping a 70/30 split of your weight into the front/back leg. Once your back knee kisses the ground or your front knee is at 90 degrees, push back up to standing. The key form focus here is that your hips move up and down like they are a lift. To progress difficulty here, the front or back foot can be elevated, or you can add dumbbells to increase the load.

Another variation for knee strength would be a box squat. Squatting with a box allows greater control and also allows the runner to load the weight on in a controlled fashion. Start with a box slightly higher than your 90-degree squat position. If at home, this could be a dining room chair or likewise and hold some weight in your hands. This could be cans from the cupboard or two large bottles of water. With a set of your weighted items whatever they may be, lower yourself down from standing to the box, pause for 2–4 seconds before driving yourself, with the weight, back to standing. This exercise forces the glutes and quads to activate on the upwards movement and target the muscles used when we push off the ground for each running stride. For both these exercises, aim for anywhere from 2–4 sets of 8–12 reps, based on your strength goals, increasing the weight week on week.

Stretches for the knees usually focus around the quad region, so a standing quad stretch will be ideal to remove most tension off of the knees. Grab your right foot with your right hand behind you and pull your heel to your buttock. In this position, making sure you are standing tall and pushing the hips forwards will deepen the stretch further. Hold for 20–30 seconds each side. Repeat twice each side. Muscles work in pairs, so make sure whenever you are addressing a weakness or tightness at the front of the body, you are also considering the muscles behind it. In this case, the hamstrings. Making sure they are loose and not too tight or weak will impact the function and outcome of your knee pain.

A stretch which can be performed to help is the hamstring sweep. Step one leg forwards, lift the front of the foot so your heel is all that's on the ground, whilst keeping that same leg straight. Leaning into your kneecap will mobilize the hamstrings. This can be done in a sweeping motion also, to aid dynamic mobility further.

Hip Pain

WHAT IS IT?

Hip pain, as with all of these terms, can cover a wide spectrum of injuries. With relation to running, the exercises I'm giving below will look to improve common hip injuries runners suffer from: piriformis syndrome and hip flexor discomfort.

HOW DOES IT HAPPEN?

Focusing on piriformis syndrome first, it can occur due to excessive tension through the lower back and glutes which causes compression of the nerves that run through the piriformis muscle. This muscle sits deep in your buttock. Lack of stretching and mobility can be a cause for this injury flaring up.

Hip flexor pain can come from weakness in the hip flexors and not necessarily the tightness we all assume. It may also occur from calf weakness, as the hip flexors help to pull the foot up after every stride. If our calves can't produce the power to do so efficiently, the hips will kick in to compensate.

WHAT EXERCISES CAN HELP?

Firstly, it's worth knowing that, in conjunction with knee strengthening work, hip strength can actually improve knee injury prevention for the future.[1] So doing both variations of knee and hip exercises can really prevent reoccurring issues. The pelvis benefits, as does the rest of the body with isometric strength.

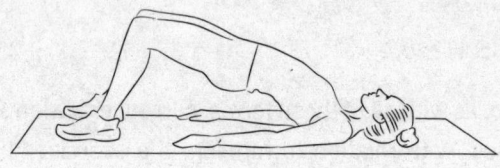

Isometric strength is strength built while holding movements. For example, hold a squat or a lunge position for a set amount of time. For hip strength, a great exercise to use it the glute bridge hold.

This exercise can be performed with or without a band,

depending on the difficulty you wish to elicit. If with a band, place it above your knees before lying down with feet flat on the ground and bent knees. From this position, we are going to drive our hips, squeezing the glutes and if with a band, drive the knees outwardly against it. The goal is that there is a straight line from the tops of the knees through the pelvis and lower spine. Progressively the time held can be increased. Start at 20 seconds and build in time over weeks as well as adding or increasing the tension on the resistance band.

An exercise to aid hip flexor strength can also be performed lying down and is known as the banded psoas march. Place the band around both your feet while lying on your back. Alternating legs, slowly draw the knee into your chest while maintaining lower back contact with the ground and having tension on the band. Repeat for 2–3 sets of 8–10 reps each side with a short 60 second rest between sets.

For hips, the gluteus maximus muscle (buttock) can become very tight from running and our day-to-day lifestyle. One of my favourite stretches for this muscle is the elevated pigeon.

Using a box or bench at your desired height, rotate your front thigh so that the knee faces outwards from the body, and keep your shin planted on said box/bench. Have the other leg straight out behind you as you drop the hips towards the ground and support your body with your hands. Keep the spine neutral to isolate the stretch to the hips. Take 3–5 deep breaths or hold for 20–30 seconds and switch sides.

These exercises mentioned only scratch the surface of problems and issues that can arise. As you've seen, many injuries stem from overuse and poor running form. It reiterates my goal for you, which is to learn and listen to your body. The more you understand your strengths, weaknesses and limitations, the better equipped you can be to keep your body strong and run ready.

Strength Sessions

With strength at the forefront of your mind, you might be thinking, well, I know I need strength but what should a session look like and how would I carry it out? I've got your back. Below is a plan to help you build your confidence in your body by completing strength training. This plan has eight weeks of strength training which can be completed no matter what kit you have. There will be a selection of exercises, each with a corresponding QR code that will link you to videos that show you exactly how each movement should be carried out. Each column within this plan offers you a workout based on the kit you have available.

AT HOME, NO KIT (BANDS ONLY): This option is for those of you working out at home. If you have no kit, I suggest accessing bands for a small expense. This way you have access to simple resistance.

IN GYM/HOME DUMBBELLS ONLY: This plan is specifically for those who want and have access to use dumbbells. This could be at home or in the gym.

IN GYM/ACCESS ALL KIT: This option is for those with a membership to a gym or all-access home kit. Looking at barbell lifts, dumbbells and kettlebell access, also.

Each session will begin with mobility, then move into activating and waking up the muscles, before strength-specific and accessory work. Each session should take no long than 45–60 minutes. If you are short on time, always look to mobilize and activate but then choose either strength or unilateral work, and then accessories.

My suggestion for each session is that session 1 is to be completed once a week, and session 2 to also be completed once a week. Session 1 is lower-body focused, and session 2 has more of a focus on upper body, back and core. For strength to have a notable effect, we want to repeat the session for four to six weeks, making small changes to weight or repetitions of the exercise.

Key terms:
- **DB**: Dumbbell
- **KB**: Kettlebell
- **RPE**: Rate of perceived exertion. This is on scale of 1–10 where 1 is easy, minimal exertion and 10 is maximal, all-out effort.
- **Reps**: Repetitions. The number of times you complete the exercise.
- **Sets**: The number of times you complete the set rep number given.
- **Rest**: Time to recover, walk or sit in these recoveries.
- **2–2–1–1**: This is the speed at which you will perform the exercise to create time under tension. Each number represents seconds, and the order corresponds to:
    1. **Eccentric phase (lowering)** – e.g. 2 seconds to lower in a squat.
    2. **Pause at the bottom** – e.g. 2-second hold at the bottom of the squat.
    3. **Concentric phase (lifting)** – e.g. 1 second to stand back up.
    4. **Pause at the top** – e.g. 1 second before starting the next rep.
- **3–1–1–0**: This is the speed at which you will perform the exercise to create time under tension. Each number represents seconds, and the order corresponds to:

1. **Eccentric phase (lowering)** — e.g. 3 seconds to lower in a squat.
2. **Pause at the bottom** — e.g. 1-second hold at the bottom of the squat.
3. **Concentric phase (lifting)** — e.g. 1 second to stand back up.
4. **Pause at the top** — e.g. 0 seconds before starting the next rep.

- **CTF:** Chest to Floor

Weeks 1–4

SESSION 1

IN GYM/ACCESS ALL KIT	IN GYM/HOME DUMBBELLS ONLY	AT HOME, NO KIT (BANDS ONLY)
Mobilize	**Mobilize**	**Mobilize**
World's Greatest Stretch	World's Greatest Stretch	World's Greatest Stretch
Squat & Reach	Squat & Reach	Squat & Reach
90/90	90/90	90/90
Activate/Prime – 3 sets	**Activate/Prime – 3 sets**	**Activate/Prime – 3 sets**
10 Banded Hip Thrusts	10 Banded Hip Thrusts	10 Banded Hip Thrusts
10 Banded Air Squats	10 Banded Air Squats	10 Banded Air Squats
20–40 sec Split Squat hold, each side	20–40 sec Split Squat hold, each side	20–40 sec Split Squat hold, each side
Strength*	**Strength***	**Strength***
Squat & Hinge	*Squat & Hinge*	*Lower focus*
3–5 sets of 10 Barbell Box Squats at 2–2–1–1**	3–5 sets of 10 DB Box Squats at 2–2–1–1**	3–5 sets of 10 Banded Squats
Rest 2 min after each set	*Rest 2 min after each set*	3–5 sets of 5/5 Monster Walks
3–5 sets of 10 Single-leg Romanian Deadlifts at 3–1–1–0	3–5 sets of 10 Single-leg Romanian Deadlifts at 3–1–1–0	3–5 sets of 10 Banded Good Mornings
Rest 2 min after each set	*Rest 2 min after each set*	*Rest 2 min after each set*

IN GYM/ACCESS ALL KIT	IN GYM/HOME DUMBBELLS ONLY	AT HOME, NO KIT (BANDS ONLY)
Unilateral, Plyometrics & Core	*Unilateral, Plyometrics & Core*	*Unilateral, Plyometrics & Core*
3 sets for quality	3 sets for quality	3 sets for quality
Split Squat: 8–12 reps each side	Split Squat: 8–12 reps each side	Split Squat: 8–12 reps each side
Rest 2 min after each set	*Rest 2 min after each set*	*Rest 2 min after each set*
Explosive Jump Squat: 4–8 reps	Explosive Jump Squat: 4–8 reps	Explosive Jump Squat: 4–8 reps
Rest 2 min after each set	*Rest 2 min after each set*	*Rest 2 min after each set*
Side Plank Banded Knee Drives: 8–12 reps each side	Side Plank Banded Knee Drives 8–12 reps each side	Side Plank Banded Knee Drives: 8–12 reps each side
Rest 1 min between sets	*Rest 1 min between sets*	*Rest 1 min between sets*
Accessory work	*Accessory work*	*Accessory work*
2 sets for quality, rest 1 min between exercises	2 sets for quality, rest 1 min between exercises	2 sets for quality, rest 1 min between exercises
DB Tibialis Anterior Raise: 16 reps	DB Tibialis Anterior Raise: 16 reps	Banded Tibialis Anterior Raise: 16 reps
DB Single-leg Calf Raises: 8 reps each side	DB Single-leg Calf Raises: 8 reps each side	Eccentric Single-leg Calf Raises: 8 reps each side
Foot Doming: 60 sec each side	Foot Doming: 60 sec each side	Foot Doming: 60 sec each side
Foot Rolling: 30–60 sec	Foot Rolling: 30–60 sec	Foot Rolling: 30–60 sec

IN GYM/ACCESS ALL KIT	IN GYM/HOME DUMBBELLS ONLY	AT HOME, NO KIT (BANDS ONLY)
* With all strength work here, Week 1 start at the lower end of the rep spectrum, then every 2 weeks increase the reps by 2. So after 6 weeks, you are trying to push the same weight for 12 reps on most exercises. Now, in a gym setting you may have availability to increase weight. If this is the case, do so on the second week of the same reps, e.g. Week 1, 8 reps; Week 2, 8 reps (add weight); Week 3, 10 reps at Week 2 weight; Week 4, 10 reps (add weight), etc.	* With all strength work here, Week 1 start at the lower end of the rep spectrum, then every 2 weeks increase the reps by 2. So after 6 weeks, you are trying to push the same weight for 12 reps on most exercises.	* With all strength work here, Week 1 start at the lower end of the rep spectrum, then every 2 weeks increase the reps by 2. So after 6 weeks, you are trying to push the same resistance band but for higher repetitions. If you have access to higher resistance of band options, then the goal could also be to increase the load used across the weeks.
** Build to a box squat that is an RPE of 9. Try to use a box/bench that causes your knees to be just above 90 degrees.		

Weeks 1–4

SESSION 2

IN GYM/ACCESS ALL KIT	IN GYM/HOME DUMBBELLS ONLY	AT HOME, NO KIT (BANDS ONLY)
Mobilize	**Mobilize**	**Mobilize**
World's Greatest Stretch	World's Greatest Stretch	World's Greatest Stretch
Squat & Reach	Squat & Reach	Squat & Reach
90/90	90/90	90/90
Activate/Prime – 3 sets	**Activate/Prime – 3 sets**	**Activate/Prime – 3 sets**
10 Banded Upright Rows	10 Banded Upright Rows	10 Banded Upright Rows
10 Banded Strict Press	10 Banded Strict Press	10 Banded Strict Press
20–40 sec Hollow Hold (choose regression option in video)	20–40 sec Hollow Hold (choose regression option in video)	20–40 sec Hollow Hold (choose regression option in video)
Strength*	**Strength***	**Strength***
Press & Pull	*Press & Pull*	*Press & Pull*
3–5 sets of 5 Barbell Strict Press into 5 Barbell Push Press	3–5 sets of 5 DB Strict Press into 5 DB Push Press	3–5 sets of 10 Heavy Band Strict Press
Rest 2 min after each set	*Rest 2 min after each set*	*Rest 2 min after each set*
3–5 sets of KB 10 Single-arm Bent Over Row at 3–1–1–0	3–5 sets of 10 DB Single-arm Bent Over Row at 3–1–1–0	3–5 sets of 10 Banded Single-arm Bent Over, Row at 3–1–1–0

IN GYM/ACCESS ALL KIT	IN GYM/HOME DUMBBELLS ONLY	AT HOME, NO KIT (BANDS ONLY)
Power, Pull & Core	***Power, Pull & Core***	***Power, Pull & Core***
2–3 sets for quality	2–3 sets for quality	2–3 sets for quality
Banded Pull-ups *OR* Negative Pull-ups: if banded, 5–8 reps choose a band that allows these reps, if negatives, 3–5 reps	Banded Horizontal Lat Pulls at 3–1–1–0: 5–8 reps	Banded Horizontal Lat Pulls at 3–1–1–0: 5–8 reps
Rest 2 min after each set	*Rest 2 min after each set*	*Rest 2 min after each set*
Floor Ball Slams: 5–8 reps	CTF Burpees: 5–8 reps	CTF Burpees: 5–8 reps
Rest 2 min after each set	*Rest 2 min after each set*	*Rest 2 min after each set*
Accessory work	***Accessory work***	***Accessory work***
2 sets for quality, rest 1 min between exercises	2 sets for quality, rest 1 min between exercises	2 sets for quality, rest 1 min between exercises
DB Tibialis Anterior Raises: 16 reps	DB Tibialis Anterior Raises: 16 reps	DB Tibialis Anterior Raises: 16 reps
DB Single-leg Calf Raises: 8 reps each side	DB Single-leg Calf Raises: 8 reps each side	DB Single-leg Calf Raises: 8 reps each side
Foot Doming: 60 sec each side	Foot Doming: 60 sec each side	Foot Doming: 60 sec each side
Foot Rolling: 30–60 sec	Foot Rolling: 30–60 sec	Foot Rolling: 30–60 sec

IN GYM/ACCESS ALL KIT	IN GYM/HOME DUMBBELLS ONLY	AT HOME, NO KIT (BANDS ONLY)
* With all strength work here, Week 1 start at the lower end of the rep spectrum, then every 2 weeks increase the reps by 2. So after 6 weeks you are trying to push the same weight for 12 reps on most exercises. Now, in a gym setting you may have availability to increase weight. If this is the case, do so on the second week of the same reps, e.g. Week 1, 8 reps; Week 2, 8 reps (add weight); Week 3 10 reps at Week 2 weight; Week 4, 10 reps (add weight), etc.	* With all strength work here, Week 1 start at the lower end of the rep spectrum, then every 2 weeks increase the reps by 2. So after 6 weeks you are trying to push the same weight for 12 reps on most exercises.	* With all strength work here, Week 1 start at the lower end of the rep spectrum, then every 2 weeks increase the reps by 2. So after 6 weeks you are trying to push the same resistance band but for higher repetitions. If you have access to higher resistance of band options then the goal could also be to increase the heaviness used across the weeks.

Weeks 5–8

SESSION 1

IN GYM/ACCESS ALL KIT	IN GYM/HOME DUMBBELLS ONLY	AT HOME, NO KIT (BANDS ONLY)
Mobilize	**Mobilize**	**Mobilize**
World's Greatest Stretch	World's Greatest Stretch	World's Greatest Stretch
Squat & Reach	Squat & Reach	Squat & Reach
90/90	90/90	90/90
Activate/Prime – 3 sets	**Activate/Prime – 3 sets**	**Activate/Prime – 3 sets**
10 Banded Good Mornings	10 Banded Good Mornings	10 Banded Good Mornings
10 Banded Air Squats	10 Banded Air Squats	10 Banded Monster Walks each side
20–40 sec Banded Glute Bridge hold	20–40 sec Banded Glute Bridge hold	20–40 sec Banded Glute Bridge hold
Strength*	**Strength***	**Strength***
Squat & Hinge	*Squat & Hinge*	*Squat & Hinge*
3–5 sets of 6–8 Barbell Tempo Deadlifts at 4–2–1–1**	3–5 sets of 6–8 DB Tempo Deadlifts at 4–2–1–1**	3–5 sets of 6–8 Banded Tempo Deadlifts at 4–2–1–1**
Rest 2 min after each set	*Rest 2 min after each set*	*Rest 2 min after each set*
3–5 sets of 10 DB Goblet Cyclist Squats at 3–1–1–0	3–5 sets of 10 DB Goblet Cyclist Squats at 3–1–1–0	3–5 sets of 10 Heel-elevated Banded Squats at 3–1–1–0
Rest 2 min after each set	*Rest 2 min after each set*	*Rest 2 min after each set*

IN GYM/ACCESS ALL KIT	IN GYM/HOME DUMBBELLS ONLY	AT HOME, NO KIT (BANDS ONLY)
Unilateral, Plyometrics & Core	*Unilateral, Plyometrics & Core*	*Unilateral, Plyometrics & Core*
3 sets for quality	3 sets for quality	3 sets for quality
DB Box Step Ups with Knee Drive: 8–12 reps each side	DB Box Step Ups with Knee Drive: 8–12 reps each side	Stair Step Downs with Knee Drive: 8–12 reps each side
Rest 2 min after each set	*Rest 2 min after each set*	*Rest 2 min after each set*
Explosive Single-leg Hops: 5–10 reps each leg	Explosive Single-leg Hops: 5–10 reps each leg	Explosive Single-leg Hops: 5–10 reps each leg
Rest 2 min after each set	*Rest 2 min after each set*	*Rest 2 min after each set*
Copenhagen Plank Hold (see options in video): 15–30 sec each side	Copenhagen Plank Hold (see options in video): 15–30 sec each side	Copenhagen Plank Hold (see options in video): 15–30 sec each side
Rest 1 min after each set	*Rest 1 min after each set*	*Rest 1 min after each set*
Accessory work	*Accessory work*	*Accessory work*
2 sets for quality, rest 1 min between exercises	2 sets for quality, rest 1 min between exercises	2 sets for quality, rest 1 min between exercises
DB Tibialis Anterior Raises: 16 reps	DB Tibialis Anterior Raises: 16 reps	Tibialis Wall Raises: 16 reps
DB Single-leg Calf Raises: 8 reps each side	DB Single-leg Calf Raises: 8 reps each side	Eccentric Single-leg Calf Raises: 8 reps each side
Foot Doming: 60 sec each side	Foot Doming: 60 sec each side	Foot Doming: 60 sec each side
Foot Rolling: 30–60 sec	Foot Rolling: 30–60 sec	Foot Rolling: 30–60 sec

IN GYM/ACCESS ALL KIT	IN GYM/HOME DUMBBELLS ONLY	AT HOME, NO KIT (BANDS ONLY)
* With all strength work here, Week 1 start at the lower end of the rep spectrum, then every 2 weeks increase the reps by 2. So after 6 weeks you are trying to push the same weight for 12 reps on most exercises. Now, in a gym setting you may have availably to increase weight. If this is the case, do so on the second week of the same reps, e.g. Week 1, 8 reps; Week 2, 8 reps (add weight); Week 3 10 reps at Week 2 weight; Week 4, 10 reps (add weight), etc.	* With all strength work here, Week 1 start at the lower end of the rep spectrum, then every 2 weeks increase the reps by 2. So after 6 weeks you are trying to push the same weight for 12 reps on most exercises.	* With all strength work here, Week 1 start at the lower end of the rep spectrum, then every 2 weeks increase the reps by 2. So after 6 weeks you are trying to push the same resistance band but for higher repetitions. If you have access to higher resistance of band options then the goal could also be to increase the weight used across the weeks.

Weeks 5–8

SESSION 2

IN GYM/ACCESS ALL KIT	IN GYM/HOME DUMBBELLS ONLY	AT HOME, NO KIT (BANDS ONLY)
Mobilize	**Mobilize**	**Mobilize**
World's Greatest Stretch	World's Greatest Stretch	World's Greatest Stretch
Squat & Reach	Squat & Reach	Squat & Reach
90/90	90/90	90/90
Activate/Prime – 3 sets	**Activate/Prime – 3 sets**	**Activate/Prime – 3 sets**
10 Banded Upright Rows	10 Banded Upright Rows	10 Banded Upright Rows
10 Banded Strict Press	10 Banded Strict Press	10 Banded Strict Press
20–40 sec Hollow Hold (choose regression option in video)	20–40 sec Hollow Hold (choose regression option in video)	20–40 sec Hollow Hold (choose regression option in video)
Strength*	**Strength***	**Strength***
Press & Core	*Press & Pull*	*Press & Pull*
3–5 sets of 5 Barbell Bench Press into 5 Single-arm DB Bench Press each side	3–5 sets of 10 Single-arm DB Bench Press into 10 DB Snatches each arm	3–5 sets of 5–10 Hand Release Press-ups
Rest 2 min after each set	*Rest 2 min after each set*	*Rest 2 min after each set*
3–5 sets of DB 10–20 Single Side Bends each side at 3–1–1–0	3–5 sets of DB 10-20 Single Side Bends each side at 3–1–1–0	3–5 sets of 10 Banded Single Side Bends each side at 3–1–1–0

IN GYM/ACCESS ALL KIT	IN GYM/HOME DUMBBELLS ONLY	AT HOME, NO KIT (BANDS ONLY)
Power, Pull & Core	*Power, Pull & Core*	*Power, Pull & Core*
2–3 sets for quality	2–3 sets for quality	2–3 sets for quality
Banded Plate Pallof Press: 5–8 reps each side	Banded Pallof Press: 5–8 reps each side	Banded Pallof Press: 5–8 reps each side
Rest 2 min after each set	*Rest 2 min after each set*	*Rest 2 min after each set*
Rotational Slams: 5–8 reps each side	Banded Rotational Chops: 5–8 reps each side	Banded Rotational Chops: 5–8 reps each side
Rest 2 min after each set	*Rest 2 min after each set*	*Rest 2 min after each set*
Standing Banded Psoas March: 5–8 reps each side		
Rest 2 min after each set		
Accessory work	*Accessory work*	*Accessory work*
2 sets for quality, rest 1 min between exercises	2 sets for quality, rest 1 min between exercises	2 sets for quality, rest 1 min between exercises
Isometric Hip Adduction + Abduction: 30 sec each	Isometric Hip Adduction + Abduction: 30 sec each	Isometric Hip Adduction + Abduction: 30 sec each
Single-leg Glute Bridge Raises: 8–12 reps each side	Single-leg Glute Bridge Raises: 8–12 reps each side	Single-leg Glute Bridge Raises: 8–12 reps each side
Standing Psoas March: 5–8 reps each side	Standing Psoas March: 5-8 reps each side	Standing Psoas March: 5–8 reps each side
Foot Doming: 60 sec each side	Foot Doming: 60 sec each side	Foot Doming: 60 sec each side

IN GYM/ACCESS ALL KIT	IN GYM/HOME DUMBBELLS ONLY	AT HOME, NO KIT (BANDS ONLY)
* With all strength work here, Week 1 start at the lower end of the rep spectrum, then every 2 weeks increase the reps by 2. So after 6 weeks you are trying to push the same weight for 12 reps on most exercises. Now, in a gym setting you may have availability to increase weight. If this is the case, do so on the second week of the same reps, e.g. Week 1, 8 reps; Week 2, 8 reps (add weight); Week 3, 10 reps at Week 2 weight; Week 4, 10 reps (add weight), etc.	* With all strength work here, Week 1 start at the lower end of the rep spectrum, then every 2 weeks increase the reps by 2. So after 6 weeks you are trying to push the same weight for 12 reps on most exercises.	* With all strength work here, Week 1 start at the lower end of the rep spectrum, then every 2 weeks increase the reps by 2. So after 6 weeks you are trying to push the same resistance band but for higher repetitions. If you have access to higher resistance of band options then the goal could also be to increase the heaviness used across the weeks.

FINDING INSPIRATION

Who makes you want to get out and move? Who helps you to find the inner willpower to move and want to be better? Your running journey will be fuelled by inspiration, and that inspiration can come from anywhere. Some runners find their inspiration from the best to ever do it: Olympians like Michael Johnson or Eliud Kipchoge, who have redefined limits by showing us what the human body is capable of. I'll never forget watching Kipchoge push through pain to a time never seen before in the marathon distance when he completed the Ineos 1:59 Challenge in Vienna in 2019. For optimum efficiency, he was flanked in a triangular formation by his team to protect and shield him from the elements. They looked like warriors ready to sacrifice themselves for their leader, having put in the work to get to the final few kilometres. Eliud was professionally poised, controlled and cruising through the streets. He had a pained but bold, optimistic grin gleaming from his face as he tore down the final kilometre of the course. Watching him know that victory was in sight, in those final few metres, and that he was to be the first man under that elusive two-hour barrier was so inspiring for me.

I couldn't wait to get out for my next run, and after watching, it was enough to light a fire in any runner's heart. Eliud is one of a kind but remember, inspiration isn't just found in the elite ranks. It's in the training partners who show up every morning, no matter the weather. It's in the single parent who laces up after years away from running, determined to start again. It's in the seventy-eight-year-old refusing to hang up their running shoes just yet. Look around your own community, and you'll find everyday runners achieving incredible things. Inspiration can also come from within. That moment when you push through a tough mile, surprise yourself with a new personal best or simply feel the joy of moving – those moments remind you why you run.

Sometimes inspiration isn't easy to come by. Especially if you're just starting out. When I embark on a new goal with my running, my motivation lasts for a good few weeks, and I'm excited to show up and push through sessions. But creeping past that two- to three-week mark, the mental walls start to build. The first few can be easy to break through. For example, not wanting to go out and run in the rain and squelch your way back through the front door – that has been me many a time. The compromise? Stay inside and run in the gym or cross-train with an indoor workout instead. You are dry, you still get the work done and there are no soggy socks. As with any plan, as the sessions become harder, the will to keep showing up can be difficult – your 'why' is really being tested. In these moments, I draw on people who inspire me. I try to surround myself with, or read, things that will reignite that will to achieve inside me. In this chapter, I've spoken to a group of phenomenal people and leaders in the international running space who, through their experiences, will hopefully become a new-found source of inspiration for you.

Running to Sobriety

For many, alcohol can have a negative effect on their lives. For some, it serves as a crutch to get through difficult times, and the battle and dependence that can follow can be devastating. For others, it may not be a crutch but something that brings on those awful hangovers and anxiety the day after a night out. Sober curiosity has continued to rise over the last five to ten years, with recent studies carried out in Australia suggesting that global sales of low- and no-alcohol products are surging.[1] The idea of quitting alcohol has helped many improve not only their health and lives but also their running.

LUCY SPRAGGAN

First up to inspire us is Lucy Spraggan. I met Lucy in 2021 when I worked on a gait analysis for her running shoes, and we've been chatting about running ever since. Lucy is an incredible singer, songwriter and artist, most well known for her time on *The X Factor*. She's had international tours, performed multiple times at Glastonbury and collaborated with some of the world's most successful artists, including Robbie Williams. Here's a look at Lucy's relationship with running:

How did you find running – or how did it find you?

'I'd been sober for around six months when I decided to take a trip to Las Vegas with friends to see if the sobriety would withstand. It did, but in the mornings when my friends were snoozing off hangovers, I felt this sudden – and never witnessed before – urge to run. So, I did! My first run was 2.4km, and I hated every second of it.'

Has it been a vehicle for helping you process big situations in your life? If so, how?

'Absolutely. The world is a lot quieter when I run. It empowers me in so many ways and assists my mental processing so much. Despite always listening to something on a run (music on a short run, podcasts or books for long runs), my brain is always ticking away in the background, digesting information.'

Has your relationship with running changed over the years? How?

'Running is a non-negotiable now, and it's a signifier of negative things if I have not been running for a period of time. It tells me that I'm overloaded or overstressed. Running is my outlet, and if I can't find the time or motivation for it, then something is wrong. I used to be bothered about how fast or far I could run, now I relish in the freedom of movement over anything else and what it does for my brain.'

What has running helped you run towards?

'Running taught me about discipline. About keeping on going even when you don't want to. It taught me to slow down the pace if I'm struggling and to stop comparing my finishing time to everyone else's. Many of the lessons from running are transferable to life in general – like the more effort you put into running, the easier it gets. It's helped me run towards self-improvement.'

SABRINA PACE-HUMPHREYS

Sabrina Pace-Humphreys is a woman who is many things. In her own words, she says, 'I am here to change societal perceptions of people who don't necessarily "fit the mould."' She's a mother, a grandmother, a motivational public speaker and presenter, a trail-running ultra-runner, an author, a social justice activist, co-founder and trustee of the community and campaigning charity Black Trail Runners, a run coach and a personal trainer. Sabrina talks about how we can not only survive but *thrive* because of our circumstances, not despite them.

How did you find running – or how did it find you?
'I only got into running when I had my fourth child – the main reason was I was really postnatally depressed. Throughout my adult life, my high levels of anxiety fed into periods of depression, which I'd mask. I'm a recovering alcoholic, so I would mask with drinking. And in 2009, I went into this really dark episode of postnatal depression where I was like, I can't live this life any more. I'm a mum. I don't want to be around the baby; I don't want to do my business; I don't want to be here. I don't know how to escape.

I went to my doctor, and it was in that conversation she suggested I try something that gets me outdoors, like running. I questioned it, but thought, well, she's a doctor. She's telling me to try jogging. I should at least try it. And I did! It was me, my milk-filled boobs, the baggy clothes I wore and the Dunlop shoes. It was so hard. But during that run, as hard as it was, I didn't have any suicidal ideation thoughts for 45 minutes. I had 45 minutes where the only thing I tuned into was moving my body forwards. Breathe, Sabrina, breathe.'

Has it been a vehicle in helping you process big situations in your life? If so, how?
'Running has been my survival tool. It's helped me process everything – from postnatal depression, to alcoholism, to the feeling of not belonging as a mixed-race woman in a predominantly white space. It has helped me move through grief, anxiety and self-doubt. It gave me something to focus on when I felt like I was drowning.

When I started, I didn't know what I was doing. I'd go online, print out a training plan, follow it, and bit by bit, I got stronger. I was keeping my results in a little notebook, seeing progress, proving to myself that I could do hard things. But it wasn't just about running – it was about what running was giving me. A purpose. A way to feel alive again. And as I got deeper into it, I realized it wasn't just my personal therapy – it was something I could use to help others feel like they belonged, too.'

Has your relationship with running changed over the years? How?

'At first, it was a way to survive, to fight my demons. Then I got caught up in it – I wanted to get faster, to train more, to do what I thought would make me a 'better' runner. But I was breaking myself, and it took the joy out of running. I was comparing myself to others, and I lost sight of why I started in the first place. Then I found trail running, and it changed everything. It was like being a beginner again.

On the trails, pace goes out the window. It doesn't matter how fast you go when you're running up a mountain or through mud – you just have to listen to your body. That's what brought the joy back to me. Now, running isn't just something I do – it's who I am. It's my way of making change. That's why I co-founded Black Trail Runners – because I saw a space where people like me didn't exist, and I wanted to change that. Running has evolved from something I needed for myself to something I now use to create space for others.'

What has running helped you run towards?

'Running has helped me run towards strength. Towards resilience. Towards knowing that I am enough exactly as I am. It's helped me run towards self-acceptance, healing and empowerment. I'm a mum of four, a grandmother, a mixed-race woman in a space where I wasn't supposed to belong. And yet, I've run across deserts, climbed mountains and stood on start lines where no one else looked like me. It's also helped me run towards the community. Towards creating something bigger than myself.

Black Trail Runners was born out of the realization that people like me weren't seen in trail running, and I knew that had to change. Representation matters. It's not just about me – it's about the next generation seeing that they belong, too. Most of all, running has helped me run towards freedom. The freedom to be who I am, unapologetically. The freedom to carve out my own space. The freedom to move forwards, one step at a time, no matter how hard it gets.'

Running to Foster Community

Running in groups has been proven to help you stay consistent in working towards your goals. Being supported – both literally, with someone running beside you, and collectively, through the shared group mentality – makes running groups and crews uniquely powerful. If you're looking for inspiration to find your own club or crew, I hope these next voices can guide and empower you. I had the pleasure of sharing conversations with some of these global changemakers.

CHARLIE DARK, MBE

I first met Charlie in the 2010s, when I'd just begun my running journey. As a Nike Pacer, I was involved in many elevated running activations within the London community, where I learned of him and of Run Dem Crew. When I think about community, his story is the first I feel compelled to share with you.

How did you find running – or how did it find you?

'Running has a habit of finding you when you need it most, and it definitely arrived in my life at a time when I was in desperate need of its powers. A painful, ten-minute Christmas-Day shuffle turned into the catalyst for a crew and a global movement.'

How did Run Dem Crew come to be, and how has running culture changed you?

'I fell in love with running and wanted to share it with as many of my friends as possible, but I knew that it needed a remix to land with the people I wanted to reach. Run Dem Crew was my attempt at creating a running club that my friends would go to. A weekly meet-up where people from my creative and musical communities could connect in person at a time when social media was on the rise. I never imagined that it would be as successful or influential as it has been over the years, but of all of the communities I've built, it's the one I'm most proud of. Bringing people together to achieve the impossible is infectious.

Running culture has introduced me to people all over the world and has opened doors to opportunities and travel that I would never have experienced if it wasn't for creating Run Dem. I've learned how to be a leader, and it's definitely helped me double down on my community-building skills. My friendship group is a better place for having discovered running.'

Has your relationship with running changed over the years? How?

'When I first started, and the feeling of impostor syndrome was high, it was through the lens of healing through performance, and I pushed myself quite hard. Over the years, particularly post-pandemic, it's become much more about connection and social interactions than chasing PBs.'

What has running helped you run towards?

'Definitely a better version of myself. It's taught me how to smile and given me a confidence that is pretty unstoppable. My self-worth radically improved once running entered into my orbit.'

CONNOR MINNEY

In 2023, Clare and I joined a run club called Gayns, founded by Connor Minney. Every Saturday, we'd meet and run the streets of London as a gaggle of road runners doing what we love: running. Connor is a fitness coach who worked in London for a decade as a Master Trainer at the well-known fitness studio Barry's Bootcamp, before starting his first business, GRNDHOUSE, a boutique fitness studio and app. Gayns, his second venture, was created to help gay people build a better relationship with themselves and the queer community. I caught up with Connor to understand how running has changed him and why he founded Gayns.

Why running, and how has it changed you?

'When I was a kid at school, I was the gay kid and crap at sports, I hated PE and I wasn't friends with any boys. But the Bleep Test (remember that?!) was the one thing I *was* good at. I remember battling it out down to the final two against one of the football boys – and I won. So I've always had a positive association with running since then. It helped me develop an understanding that sport wasn't my thing, but fitness was, and my confidence grew from there. Working at Barry's, I taught treadmill running to music – which I absolutely loved – and learned through that I could really transform people's relationship with themselves, tap in to their potential and empower them. Now I have a run club through Gayns, and during a really tough period of my life it's really helped me find community and connection.'

When and why was Gayns born?

'Gayns was born originally at the beginning of 2022 as a one-to-one online coaching solution for queer people to build a better relationship with training, nutrition and, in turn, their bodies. I wasn't able to be paid from my first business, so it really started as a side hustle to pay the rent. Then at the beginning of 2023, when that first business failed, I focused my efforts more on Gayns as a way to overcome all the negative emotions that came with that failure and sink my teeth into something that felt like it had more social impact.

I started the run club in February 2023, and it went from thirty people in the first week to 160 people a few months later, so it really felt like it was needed! Being queer myself and having always worked in fitness, I knew the specific cultural afflictions that we have when it comes to ourselves, our bodies and the way we show up in the community, so I wanted to create a space that kind of dissolved a lot of that.'

Why can being queer and showing up in running spaces feel hard?

'Being a minority in a very hetero-dominated industry can be a point of fear or intimidation for queer people. Run clubs offer more opportunity to connect with people than, say, a fitness class or gym session, but turning up to a straight run club and not feeling as if you identify with the others in the group, or wondering if it's members even agree with LGBTQ+ people's rights and existence, can feel challenging, especially if it's your first time.

Sure, queer people can go to any run club – the straight-dominated ones aren't queer exclusionary – but a run club is often about identity, which is why a lot of run clubs have specific niches or clear demographics in attendance. Its members want to meet like-minded individuals, potential suitors and friends in the process, so creating a space where you can facilitate this is imperative. Sport and fitness can often be a point of trauma or shame for a lot of queer people from the days of PE at school, so creating a space where those people can form a new relationship with it, surrounded by others with the same experience is incredibly important.'

What has running helped you run towards?
'Running has helped me run towards finding community and connection with others in the LGBTQ+ space in a totally different way.'

CORY WHARTON-MALCOLM

I have worked with and learned my craft from some formidable coaches. During my time with NRC (Nike Run Club), one who will always stand out to me as someone who made running fun and interactive was Cory. Cory ('Bit Beefy' as some also know him), is an Apple Fitness+ trainer, author, coach and run-crew founder. He helped me understand how we can play in our own environments. To use parks and even lampposts or traffic lights to engage our minds and bodies in running alongside our peers.

How did you find running – or how did it find you?
'I stumbled across running, or should I say running came and found me. I'd lived in London my whole life and watched the London Marathon on television many times, but I'd never been to see it in person. My friend ran it, so I went to watch and cheer her on. After witnessing London come and cheer for complete strangers, I was hooked. I said: 'Next year I wanna run this.' My friends laughed, which added a little extra gas to the fire. So even if I hadn't been fully committed, I certainly was then. I started running the following week.'

Has it been a vehicle in helping you process big situations in your life? If so, how?

'Since finding running, it's been like a Swiss Army knife that appears to be able to solve problems for me. Or should I say, having running gives me the time and space I need to process things. Whether it's thirty minutes or two hours, that's free time on the road for my brain to work through whatever it wants or I want. This sometimes happens without me even knowing. When I first found running, I was still grieving at the loss of my grandmother, and to be honest, I don't think I would have found the peace that I did without running.'

Has your relationship with running changed over the years? How?

'Running just used to be the thing that I did. It started off as just putting one foot in front of the other to prepare for a marathon. It was this struggle purely to prove a point to other people. Then it became about myself physically, then it was about my mental health and relationship with food and opening up to people. It became my therapist, a way to test and push myself, my community builder, my passport to the rest of the world, then my creative partner, then work, a means by which I was able to change the trajectory of my life and those in my community. Now running is everything all at once.'

How was Track Mafia, as well as connections with international run crews, born?

'Track Mafia was born out of a want and need to learn more about what would happen if we were really intentional about the way that we trained. It was about taking what we had learned from running on the roads and adapting it to the track, which if you think about it, is kinda the reverse of how it normally happens.

I was introduced to Charlie Dark who founded Run Dem Crew. I set up Run Dem Crew West as per Charlie's request and ran it with Ellie Wood. Many of the sessions I built out on the road were about using the roads as a track. So, I didn't see a street with lampposts, I saw a track with built-in places for gradual acceleration. I didn't see a multi-storey car park, I saw a perfect location for hill reps and quick descents, and a football stadium wasn't just a place to watch football – the perimeter was the perfect 1k or 1 mile rep. There I met Jules and Jeggi. The three of us trained a lot together and noticed that we really loved doing anything that made us stronger, more efficient, smarter runners. We loved speed sessions, tempos, intervals, fartlek and learning about the craft. We read more, watched more and started to experiment more. The three of us started our track sessions at Paddington Recreation Ground track on Thursday, the same place that RDCWest would meet on a Monday.

The goal was to really learn how to build out sessions that worked for us – fun, but a lot of hard work – sessions that would help us really get used to embracing discomfort. In the beginning, it wasn't about other people – just us. People saw what we were doing and literally asked if they could join us. Three became four, four became five, five became ten and so on.

We always made it very clear to people that this was *our*

session, and you were welcome to join us. As far as connections with international running crews [go], it was Charlie Dark who introduced me to other crews around the world who were doing similar things with running and culture in their own cities. We all bonded over a love of music, art, food, fashion, community and collective understanding that running was boring, but it was ultimately that that had brought us together. We would meet in different countries for races, and the host crew in whatever city we were in would show us their world. From that, lifelong bonds and friendships were forged. Now, because of spending all those years going from race to race, city to city, I have running friends all over the world – even though we might not even run with each other any more.'

What has running helped you run towards?
'It's helped me run towards a better version of myself, a version that I didn't know existed. It's helped me run towards friends, family and community. It's helped me run towards a better relationship with myself and my mental health. Running has given me exactly what I needed, at times, it wasn't what I wanted, but that's just like life, right?'

Running Because Your Body CAN

One of the hardest things about running can be that as you progress, injury can arise. There can be a daunting moment when the thing you love to do is taken away from you. With every day that passes, as you rest to heal, a niggling doubt can creep in – that you may never run at your best again, or even worse, that you might get injured again. These women talk about how both community and injury made them appreciate running more than ever before.

KIRSTEN FERGUSON

Kirsten Ferguson is one of my favourite Peloton instructors. She's strong-minded and has overcome so many difficulties in life, including during her Peloton career – most notably, undergoing hip surgery and having the fear of whether she would even be able to run again. As president and CEO of the 'Ratchet Moms Club' in the Peloton community, her energy is contagious. Her intention-setting Sunday walk empowers everyone not just to tackle the week, but to conquer their lives – the energy we all need. I had to speak with her to understand what running, overcoming injury and community mean to her.

How has the Peloton community changed your life?
'I joined Peloton in 2015 after I had my first daughter. At a time in my life where I was walking through postpartum and falling back in love with this stronger body I have (I say stronger because it just created a human and it was much different than what it was before). The Peloton community was a space that I felt welcomed and supported [in]. The community is truly family.'

For those afraid to join a community space due to intimidation or fear of judgement, what advice would you give?

'For those afraid to join the community I would say . . . Why do you feel that way? Understanding the driving factor of our fear is key information. I would say, start small first and let this community completely surprise you. It has for me.'

How do you believe the online fitness space can encourage people to start running, and what is your own experience?

'The online fitness community gives you a greater opportunity to build community and meet people for where you are at in your fitness level! It also gives you the ability to make different connections around the world. It is really such a beautiful connection to witness and be a part of.'

How did having your hip injury change your appreciation for running?

'I learned so much about myself and my body. I learned the importance of warming up and recovery. I learned first hand the importance of strength training and training specifically for running. Once I did all of that I realized, oh wow I can do this running thing and I can do it without being in pain. I suffered so much because I just wasn't training properly.'

What does running mean to you?

'Running to me has become a beautiful space where I'm continuing to surprise myself. Running is such a beautiful journey that is ever-changing, and you must always respond to it with grace and gratitude. Not every run is going to be a great run, but even a stumble is a step forwards and I'm grateful for it.'

JOSLYN THOMPSON RULE

My coach and friend Joslyn Thompson Rule is a personal trainer and sports therapist. She's formerly a Nike Global Master trainer and is currently a tread and strength instructor for Peloton. She also shares her words of wisdom as the host of her podcast, *Listen Loudly*.

How does being a sports therapist impact how you began and continue your running journey?
'For me, I'm always looking at it from several angles. Rehabbing people taught me how disconnected people are from their bodies. (It's why I tell people to tune in so much when I'm teaching – the dialogue you have with yourself is so important.) I don't really buy in to limitations because of age (within reason), and so I think I train a lot smarter now than before, I probably enjoy and trust the process more, too. And I'm a lot more patient! This helps, a lot.'

Over the years, from those you've worked with, why do you see runners specifically getting injured?
'Often because running itself is the sole focus with less attention given to strength training or giving enough time to recover. And with that, not enough information around how strength

247

training and recovery practices can enhance running. Truly both are a form of injury prevention, on top of impacting running performance positively.'

How do you believe the online fitness space can encourage people to start running, and what is your own experience?

'In terms of social media, running – specifically run clubs – appeals from not just a movement perspective but from a social perspective also. Not only do you run but you can meet like-minded people doing the same and from there forge new relationships. As a whole, the online fitness space has given people greater access to movement – and yet, much still requires home-gym equipment or access to a fitness space. Running doesn't and so is the most accessible of all, if you are able bodied. For many people there is still this mental block of "I'm not a runner", as many think it is defined around racing or speed/distance. If someone has no desire to run, cool, but if someone feels they're not worthy of being a runner, it is my job to guide them through a manageable process to get them there. So much about movement and exercise is understanding the steps and process, and the meaning we give to it all. I help people to navigate that, twenty-one years of coaching has allowed me to be clear on that process and its application.'

How has the Peloton community changed your life?

'What drives me as a coach is to see people accomplish things, big and small, that they didn't think they could. Peloton has given me access to millions of people so that I can continue to do that. I now hear incredible stories daily about how movement has impacted others, again in small and/or life-changing ways. How they rally together not only to support me, but especially each other, is amazing!'

For those afraid to join a community space due to intimidation or fear of judgement, what advice would you give?

'I would say that we are very good at convincing ourselves of a lot of things we are not, or cannot do – it's how we protect ourselves, and with good reason. The easiest solution – bring a friend. You don't have to show up by yourself, and if you do, familiarize yourself with the coach, tell them you are new and [ask] if there is anyone they could pair you up with. A good coach will do that for you.'

What has running helped you run towards?

'At different points in my life, for the most part, it has shown me possibility, mostly of my physical capacity – when it flows regardless of speed/distance it is often a reflection of my life being in flow and or in smooth motion. It's one of my check-in markers of how much or little I'm taking care of myself. Avoiding injury is something I strive for every runner to have at the forefront of their training. Being healthy and running well [are] of the highest importance. Understanding that the health I refer to isn't just physical but mental and emotional also.'

Running Towards Representation

Running when you see people who look like you can be an instant reminder that not only can you do it, but you are welcomed in the running space and world. As you know from my story, being able to see someone who looked like me supported my desire to strive towards my childhood goal. In the next few interviews, I hope you will feel seen and heard by those trying to make a space for you.

KAYLA JETER

Kayla Jeter is a multifaceted leader: coach, athlete, host and speaker. A former pro volleyball player turned endurance runner, Kayla advocates for accessible wellness. Her expertise has been featured in top publications, and she's built a community of over 150,000 engaged followers online.

Why running, and how has it changed you?

'I fell into running through my 100MilesofSummer challenge, stayed for the people, and through it have uncovered my limitless, label-less potential. Participating in a homogenous sport presents many opportunities for doubt to creep in of "not belonging" or "being good enough". But for me, I grew up both feeling and literally being othered, whether it's on a race course or a weekend jog, I take up space as a Black woman with an athletic build at 5'10" with so much pride. When I tore my ACL [Anterior Cruciate Ligament — the ligament that stabilizes the knee during twisting or sudden movements] in college, I was told I'd never be able to run a marathon; not that I wasn't capable but because the training would be too tough on my joints. Five marathons, two ultra-marathon relays, one ultra-marathon and one six-day ultra-marathon running over 234 miles later, I'm proving just how capable and built for this I am.

At the end of the day, it's just running but it has the potential to give and uncover so much more.'

When and why was 100MilesofSummer born?

'100MilesofSummer was created in May 2018, my first Chicago summer, as a way to get to know the city more intimately by foot (the best way to explore any city!), but [it] became the healing space for my relationship with running. An exploration of inner and outer landscapes, which invited me to transform my relationship with a movement so primal that had primarily been used for punishment throughout my athletic career. The challenge is simple: walk, jog, run or wheel 100 miles between 1 May and 31 August for better health. 100MilesofSummer is a global community health initiative.

What started with twelve former collegiate athletes ripping 5ks during their lunch breaks, silly racing to be first on the virtual scoreboard, blossomed and boomed to a diverse community of over 270,000 participants worldwide – the majority of which don't come from a consistent running background and through the challenge have built healthier habits extending their health span, built body confidence, found their community and collectively challenged the narrative of what a runner "looks like" to be one reflective of all body sizes, shapes, colours and abilities.'

To those scared or intimidated by running, what advice would you share?

'You don't have to run a marathon to be a runner. Heck, you don't have to race a day in your life. You don't have to run on the road to be a runner; you can explore the trails or a new city [on] foot. You don't have to have a flashy kit to be a runner; you really just need a good pair of shoes that best fit you. You don't have to run fast to be a runner; you just have to show up and put one foot in front of their other at a forwards pace: left foot, right foot, breathe.'

DORA ATIM

Dora Atim is a fearless advocate for women's empowerment, especially championing Black women in sports as a catalyst for unlocking their full potential. Bold, unapologetic and deeply authentic, she believes in breaking barriers while looking good doing it. Through her work, she inspires women to step into their power, own their space and redefine success on their own terms.

How did running become your chosen sport, especially trail?

'Trail running became my chosen sport during the lockdown in 2020, but my first experience with it was nearly a decade earlier. Back in 2011, while living in West London, I stumbled onto the trails and was struck by how beautiful and calming it felt – like stepping into another world. But at the time, my biggest takeaway wasn't the peace it gave me; it was the frustration of muddy trainers that I either had to clean or, in my case, replace. I didn't realize then that trail running would find its way back to me when I needed it most.

Fast forward nine years, and the world was in turmoil. The weight of the Black Lives Matter movement, the collective grief over Ahmaud Arbery – who was murdered while simply out on a run – left me emotionally and mentally drained. I found myself questioning how I existed in the running space, whether I truly belonged and where I could find solace. The only thing that kept me moving forwards was the trails.

I remember one moment so vividly . . . standing in the middle of a forest, after pushing through the weight of despair, listening to a carefully curated house music playlist. And then, something shifted. I felt joy. I felt hope. I felt free. Tears streamed down my face, not from pain, but from the sheer release of it all. In that moment, I knew I had to do something with this feeling, to create something that would allow others to experience this same sense of belonging and liberation.

And so, Ultra Black Running was born. A space where Black women, Black non-binary people and anyone who has ever felt unseen in outdoor spaces could come as they are – unapologetically, joyfully and without question.'

What does representation in running look like to you? Was this where UBR came from?

'Trail running and distance running make me feel alive. They ground me, free me and push me beyond what I ever thought I was capable of. But my love for running didn't come from running itself, it was unlocked by another sport – boxing. That's the power of trying something new. You never know what it might awaken in you. And that's why representation is so important.

When we see people like us doing something, it makes it feel possible. It opens doors we didn't even know were there. Representation isn't just about visibility, it's about access, belonging and the stories that shape how we see the world and our place in it. Everyone, from every walk of life, should be able to see themselves reflected, included and valued. We live in a beautiful world full of incredible people, but if those stories aren't told, how will we ever truly see each other?

Ultra Black Running was born from this belief. I wanted Black women, Black non-binary people, anyone who has ever felt like outdoor spaces weren't built for them to know that they belong. No code-switching. No shrinking yourself. Just showing up as you are, unapologetically. Because the trails, the mountains and the roads should be for everyone. And if we can get more people to just try it, who knows what they might unlock in themselves?'

What is the greatest running challenge you've overcome? Why was it one of the toughest?
'My first "Did Not Finish" at an ultra-marathon hit harder than I ever expected. I thought I had prepared enough, trained, planned, visualized, but when the moment came, it wasn't enough. Letting go of my ego and accepting defeat was one of the hardest things I've ever done. But that DNF reshaped the way I see ultra-racing, and honestly, the way I see life.

In ultras, nothing is guaranteed. You can do everything "right" and still not make it to the finish. And that's the beauty of it. Every race, every run, every single kilometre is a gift. That first DNF didn't break me, it built me. It taught me to respect the distance, to embrace the uncertainty and to be deeply grateful for every step forwards, no matter how far I go.'

How has running helped you run towards yourself?
'Running has never been about running away, it's always been about running towards myself. I've always known my why, but through running, I've found the clearest way to deliver it to my community and beyond. Every step, every race, every challenge has reinforced my mission: to spark curiosity, increase participation and create space for marginalized groups in places they've too often been excluded from.

Because I'm so sure of why I do this work, running has sharpened my focus, keeping me aligned with the people, companies and organizations that share my values. It's more than movement – it's purpose in motion. And with every kilo-metre, I'm not just running; I'm building, connecting and pushing the world forwards.'

I hope this chapter has shown you the power that running has had for others, but also the effect it can have on you. Remember that everyone was once at the beginning of their journey. Even Eliud once took that first step to run and felt all those feelings you have. Lucy and Sabrina used running to keep them on track to give them purpose For Lucy, through losing the idea of comparison and focusing on her journey only. For Sabrina, to help find herself when life tried to pull her under. We can see how community plays a role in almost every runner's journey. The power of showing up and creating something initially for yourself like Charlie, who just wanted a place to bring friends together but then it transformed into a global running movement. If you struggle to show up in person, a welcoming and inclusive online community can also be there for you. Both Jos and Kirsten have been inspired by the Peloton community and how their lives have changed for the better from it. They've both learned that running shows you possibility and that even if it's a stumble forwards in some runs, it's still a step towards a better you. Finally, Kayla and Dora show us that running has created a purpose to show up for others. To create global movements to disrupt, to overcome societal and familial hardships, to empower others to move and not only that, but to celebrate that movement. I hope this has confirmed for you that running is about more that running. I hope you find your inspiration to run.

KEY TAKEAWAYS:

- Inspiration takes time. The early buzz of a new goal often fades after a few weeks. When motivation dips, drawing on stories, community and your deeper 'why' can help reignite your drive.

- Running is a form of healing. For Lucy and Sabrina, running offered mental clarity and emotional grounding during some of life's hardest moments. It became a lifeline – not for performance, but for peace.

- Pace doesn't define you – commitment does. Every runner's journey is unique. Whether you're walking, jogging or sprinting, what counts is that you're showing up and honouring your own process.

- Community keeps you going. From local run clubs to global digital platforms like Peloton, community creates accountability, joy and a shared sense of purpose. You're never really running alone.

- Representation creates belonging. Kayla, Dora and Sabrina remind us how powerful it is to see someone who looks like you in spaces you once felt excluded from. When we feel seen, we feel like we can stay.

- Running brings you closer to yourself. These stories prove that running isn't about escaping life, it's about moving through it with purpose. With every step, you're not just covering distance – you're uncovering who you are.

FINDING THE FUTURE

From the young, innocent kid who found joy, happiness and identity in running to understanding myself as an adult has been a journey — one that isn't over. I've shared the many directions that my life has taken and how running has always been my saving grace. I hope you can see how running through my grief helped me to overcome depression and see the positives in each day. How the power of the global running community helped me feel seen, heard, welcomed, and encouraged me to find my purpose.

Running can do that for you too. It's more than taking steps outside to burn calories or achieve PBs. Being a runner is part of my identity, and existing as a runner is about so much more than *just* running. Through my lens, I hope you can see how running can be used as a vehicle for change, and that you now have all the tools necessary to go out there and show up for yourself — to find moments for yourself among the challenges life throws at you and remember two simple words: you matter.

Running takes you away from wherever you are. By taking those first few steps, it moves you away from your start point, from comfort and, as I realized, from reality in the toughest moments. In running away to escape, I actually ended up running towards myself. I hope your journey is not as tumultuous as mine. I hope for you that running can become a part of and continue to enrich your life — whether that's through races, finding new communities or even just a run around your local park. Finding time for yourself is important, and you deserve it.

I'm not sure where I'm running towards next. It may be a lonely road filled with persistent storms and gale-force winds. There may be uneven, mossy terrain. There could be the highest peaks and then low, challenging troughs. That same road could lead me to an expansive and bright wilderness. I could be surrounded by others offering their hands to carry me onwards, as we all bask in the gleaming sunshine. I've no idea what's ahead of me. But what I do know is, no matter the outcome, I'm going to keep on running, and I hope you do too.

NOTES

FINDING CHANGE

1   'Brighton postcode area Census 2021', *Plumplot*, accessed 29
    July 2025, https://www.plumplot.co.uk/Brighton-census-2021.
    html#:~:text=90.9%25%20people%20are%20white%2C%20
    3.2,23.7%25%20households%20have%202%20cars.

2   'Census 2021', *Office for National Statistics*, accessed 29 July
    2025, https://www.ons.gov.uk/census/maps/choropleth/identity/
    ethnic-group/ethnic-group-tb-6a/white.

3   'Slave Trade Records from Liverpool, 1754–1792', *British Online
    Archives*, https://britishonlinearchives.com/collections/5/slave-
    trade-records-from-liverpool-1754-1792.

4   Mark Christian, 'The Fletcher Report 1930: A Historical Case
    Study of Contested Black Mixed Heritage Britishness', *Journal of
    Historical Sociology* 21 (2008), pp. 213–41. 10.1111/j.1467-
    6443.2008.00336.x

5   Kris Manjapra, 'When Will Britain Face Up to Its Crimes against
    Humanity?', *The Guardian* (2018), https://www.theguardian.com/
    news/2018/mar/29/slavery-abolition-compensation-when-will-
    britain-face-up-to-its-crimes-against-humanity.

FINDING AUTHENTICITY

1   Ilan Meyer and Laura Dean, 'Internalized Homophobia, Intimacy, and Sexual Behaviour among Gay and Bisexual Men', in *Stigma and Sexual Orientation: Understanding Prejudice against Lesbians, Gay Men, and Bisexuals*, ed. Gregory M. Herek (Thousand Oaks, CA: Sage Publications, 1998), pp. 160–186.
2   'Map of Jurisdictions That Criminalise LGBT People', Human Dignity Trust, https://www.humandignitytrust.org/lgbt-the-law/map-of-criminalisation/.

FINDING COMMUNITY

1   'Campaign to End Loneliness', *Campaign to End Loneliness*, https://www.campaigntoendloneliness.org/.
2   'What Does It Mean to Be Human?', *Smithsonian National Museum of Natural History*, https://humanorigins.si.edu/human-characteristics/social-life#:~:text=Group%20Survival
3   Rob Franken, Hidde Bekhuis, and Jochem Tolsma, 'Running Together: How Sports Partners Keep You Running', *Frontiers in Sports and Active Living* (2022), https://doi.org/10.3389/fspor.2022.643150.
4   Carolyn R. Plateau, Justine Anthony, Stacy A. Clemes, and Clare D. Stevinson, 'Prospective Study of Beginner Running Groups: Psychological Predictors and Outcomes of Participation', *Behavioural Medicine* (2022), pp. 55–62, https://doi.org/10.1080/08964289.2022.2100865.

FINDING CHALLENGE

1   A. Stephen Fadare, P. Ermalyn Lambaco, B. Yasmin Mangorsi, J. D. Louise Lorchano, and B. Juvenmile Tercio, 'A Voyage into the Visualization of Athletic Performances: A Review', *American Journal of Multidisciplinary Research and Innovation* (2022), pp. 105–109, https://doi.org/10.54536/ajmri.v1i3.479.
2   Radu Predoiu, Alexandra Predoiu, Georgeta Mitrache, Madalina

Firanescu, Germina Cosma, Gheorghe Dinuta, and Razvan Alexandru Bucuroiu, 'Visualisation Techniques in Sport – The Mental Road Map for Success', *Discobolul – Physical Education, Sport and Kinetotherapy Journal* (2020), pp. 245–256, https://doi.org/10.35189/dpeskj.2020.59.3.4.

FINDING THE START

1   Harrison Philip Crowell and Irene S. Davis, 'Gait Retraining to Reduce Lower Extremity Loading in Runners', *Clinical Biomechanics* (2011), pp. 78–83, https://doi.org/10.1016/j.clinbiomech.2010.09.003.

2   Adam I. Daoud, Gary J. Geissler, Frank Wang, Jason Saretsky, Yahya A. Daoud, and Daniel E. Lieberman, 'Foot Strike and Injury Rates in Endurance Runners: A Retrospective Study', *Medicine and Science in Sports and Exercise* (2012), pp. 1325–34, https://doi.org/10.1249/MSS.0b013e3182465115.

3   Tomas K. Tong, Alison K. McConnell, Hua Lin, Jinlei Nie, Haifeng Zhang, and Jiayuan Wang, '"Functional" Inspiratory and Core Muscle Training Enhances Running Performance and Economy', *Journal of Strength and Conditioning Research* (2016), pp. 2942–51, https://doi.org/10.1519/JSC.0000000000000656.

4   Donald F. Kessler, 'Running FASTER: Changing Running Technique to Reduce Stress Injuries', *International Journal of Athletic Therapy and Training* (2020), pp. 49–53.

5   Emma Burnett, Jenny White, and Joanna Scurr, 'The Influence of the Breast on Physical Activity Participation in Females', *Journal of Physical Activity and Health* (2015), pp. 588–94, https://doi.org/10.1123/jpah.2013-0236.

6   Peta Bee, 'Why the Jiggle Factor Is a Pain for Women', *The Times*, n.d., https://www.thetimes.com/uk/science/article/why-the-jiggle-factor-is-a-pain-for-women-tfmh3qc5xfk.

7   Benno M. Nigg, Jennifer Baltich, Stefan Hoerzer, and Hendrik Enders, 'Running Shoes and Running Injuries: Mythbusting and a Proposal for Two New Paradigms: "Preferred Movement Path" and "Comfort Filter"', *British Journal of Sports Medicine* (2015), pp. 1290–94.

FINDING THE SCIENCE OF RUNNING

1   'Basics of Anatomy: Arches of the Foot', *Moushu's Pilates*, https://moushuspilates.com/basics-of-anatomy-arches-foot/

2   Renata Woźniacka, Łukasz Oleksy, Agnieszka Jankowicz-Szymańska, Anna Mika, Renata Kielnar, and Artur Stolarczyk, 'The Association between High-Arched Feet, Plantar Pressure Distribution and Body Posture in Young Women', *Scientific Reports* (2019), https://doi.org/10.1038/s41598-019-53459-w

3   Rasmus Oestergaard Nielsen, Ida Buist, Erik Thorlund Parner, Ellen Aagaard Nohr, Henrik Sørensen, Martin Lind, and Sten Rasmussen, 'Foot Pronation Is Not Associated with Increased Injury Risk in Novice Runners Wearing a Neutral Shoe: A 1-Year Prospective Cohort Study', *British Journal of Sports Medicine* (2014), pp. 440–47, https://doi.org/10.1136/bjsports-2013-092202.

4   Amelie Werkhausen, Magne Lund-Hansen, Lucas Wiedenbruch, Klaus Peikenkamp, and Hannah Rice, 'Technologically Advanced Running Shoes Reduce Oxygen Cost and Cumulative Tibial Loading per Kilometer in Recreational Female and Male Runners', *Scientific Reports* (2024), https://doi.org/10.1038/s41598-024-62263-0.

5   Adam Tenforde, Tim Hoenig, Amol Saxena, and Karsten Hollander, 'Bone Stress Injuries in Runners Using Carbon Fiber Plate Footwear', *Sports Medicine* (2023), https://doi.org/10.1007/s40279-023-01818-z.

6   Jeppe Bo Lauersen, Ditte Marie Bertelsen, and Lars Bo Andersen, 'The Effectiveness of Exercise Interventions to Prevent Sports Injuries: A Systematic Review and Meta-analysis of Randomised Controlled Trials', *British Journal of Sports Medicine* (2014), pp. 871–77.

7   Carolina Romero Cardenas, 'The Art of Choosing the Right Running Shoe: A Review Article', *Journal of Foot and Ankle* (2024), pp. 146–55.

FINDING SPEED

1   Arran Parmar, Thomas W. Jones, and Philip R. Hayes, 'The Use of Interval-Training Methods by Coaches of Well-Trained Middle- to Long-Distance Runners', *International Journal of Strength and Conditioning* (2021), https://doi.org/10.47206/ijsc.v1i1.54.

2   Knut Sindre Mølmen, Nicki Winfield Almquist, and Øyvind Skattebo, 'Effects of Exercise Training on Mitochondrial and Capillary Growth in Human Skeletal Muscle: A Systematic Review and Meta-Regression', *Sports Medicine* (2025), pp. 115–44, https://doi.org/10.1007/s40279-024-02120-2.

FINDING STRENGTH

1   Lucas R. Nascimento, Luci F. Teixeira-Salmela, Ricardo B. Souza, and Renan A. Resende, 'Hip and Knee Strengthening Is More Effective Than Knee Strengthening Alone for Reducing Pain and Improving Activity in Individuals with Patellofemoral Pain: A Systematic Review with Meta-analysis', *Journal of Orthopaedic and Sports Physical Therapy* (2018), pp. 19–31, https://doi.org/10.2519/jospt.2018.7365.

FINDING INSPIRATION

1   Belinda Lunnay, Emily Nicholls, Amy Pennay, Sarah MacLean, Carlene Wilson, Samantha B. Meyer, Kristen Foley, Megan Warin, Ian Olver, and Paul R. Ward, 'Sober Curiosity: A Qualitative Study Exploring Women's Preparedness to Reduce Alcohol by Social Class', *International Journal of Environmental Research and Public Health* (2022), https://doi.org/10.3390/ijerph192214788.

ACKNOWLEDGEMENTS

To my mum, for being a role model to me and showing me that strong and smart women can take up space and succeed in an industry not traditionally made for them. Learning from a young age about your drive to succeed in your career laid the foundations for me to be where I am now. Thank you for selflessly showing up for me, not only when writing this book but also during the tough times I've written about in these pages. Even if I wasn't always so forthcoming with how I was really coping, having you there and guiding me while acting in both parenting roles meant the world to me. I love you.

A huge thank you to Nora and Oscar at The Millar Agency for believing in me and trusting my thoughts and ideas in the very first place. Nora, you have no idea the gratitude I have for you nagging me to send you my draft.

To Hattie, for seeing the vision and helping me fine-tune and polish the concept of this book. To Jodie and all the team at Pan Macmillan and Bluebird, for their hard work and guiding me in writing my debut book. You all made this book a reality, and for that I couldn't be more grateful.

To Cara, the most lovely, empathetic and understanding

editor I could possibly have had. All the thanks to you for hearing my experiences and helping to bring out my true inner writer. I felt safe and trusted in your editing hands.

To everyone who has helped me learn throughout the years, Paul O'Malley, Richard Felton, Dan Cracknell, Steve and Shula Wolfenden at Profeet, who cared for me like family during my time there and taught me all I know. To my close circle, who were there during the years of bringing this book to reality. Thank you for answering the calls, the voice notes, the texts and just listening. Amira, Mikki, Keziah, Laura, Gen, Hannah and my sister Temi, you don't know how many times you were a lifeline.

Dad, I believe you were guiding me over these years. I can imagine the shock in your face seeing me write this. Look at what I managed! More grease to my elbows, isn't that right? I'll always try to make you proud in all I do. Love, your little girl.

Lastly, to my soon-to-be wife Clare, thank you for showing me the power I have within myself to shine. Thank you for creating a safe space in our lives for me to write this book. You've pulled me up in some of the darkest moments. You've helped me to show up and prove fear, doubt and negative talk wrong. Love, always.